teach yourself...
Jazz Piano Comping
for cocktail, combo & big band pianists

Al Stevens
al@alstevens.com

Mockingbird Songs & Stories

Mockingbird Songs & Stories
5020 Saturday Place, Cocoa, FL 32926

Dedication

To the fond memory of Joe Piscatele, a giant

*"You can make a living playing jazz piano...
as long as you don't need a lot of money."*

Copyright © 2018 Al Stevens. No part of this publication may be reproduced in any form or by any means without the prior written permission of the author.

The tunes given as examples in this book are either the author's original compositions or well-known public domain tunes. The tune fragments that demonstrate musical theory and structure do not include melodies or lyrics. The chord changes are what you will be learning and playing. If you want to learn melodies and lyrics, which I encourage you to do, there are many recordings and *fake* and *real* books available.

Cover art inspired by the work of William Stauffer.

Edited by Jane Feitler.

ISBN-13: 978-0-9886623-9-1

Table of Contents

PART I Introduction..1
Chapter 1. Getting Started...2
   Who are You?..2
   What do You Need?...2
   What's in this Book?..4
   Reading Musical Notation..4
   The Changes..6
   Accompaniment...6
   Keyboard Span...7
   Who am I?..7
   Why the Piano?..8
   Jazz...8
   Jazz and Standards..10
   Exercises and Practicing..10
PART II Scales and Chords..11
Chapter 2. Tones, Intervals and Scales..12
   Tones..12
   Intervals..13
   Scales..14
   Summary of Scales...16
Chapter 3. Chord Basics..17
   Chords..17
   Chord Symbols...17
   Standard Symbols?...20
   The Root Note..20
   Inversions...21
   Slash Chords..21
Chapter 4. Basic Chords..23
   Major..23
   Minor..24
   Dominant 7...25
   Minor 7...26
   Other Roots..26
Chapter 5. Colorful Dominant 7 and Minor 7 Chords..30
Chapter 6. Colorful Major and Minor Chords..34
Chapter 7. Diminished Chords..38
   Cdim7, E♭dim7, G♭dim7, Adim7..38
   Fdim7, A♭dim7, Bdim7, Ddim7..39
   Gdim7, B♭dim7, D♭dim7, Edim7..40
   Dim7 Substitutions...41
   Half Diminished (min7♭5)...41
Chapter 8. Augmented and Suspended Chords...45
   Augmented...45
   Augmented 7...46
   Suspended..48

Chapter 9. Altered Interval Chords 51
Dominant 7 Flat Nine (♭9) 51
Dominant 7 Sharp Nine (♯9) 51
Dominant 7 Flat 5 (♭5) 52
Exercises 52
Chapter 10. Rootless Chords 54
PART III Music Theory 56
Chapter 11. Harmonic Contexts 57
Chord Resolution 57
The Cycle/Circle of 4ths/5ths 59
Resolving Chords 60
Chapter 12. Tonal Centers 62
Harmonic Contexts 62
PART IV The Changes 65
Chapter 13. Common Progressions 66
Two-Five 66
Two-Five-One 67
One-Six-Two-Five 74
Chapter 14. The Blues 77
Major Blues 77
Minor Blues 79
Non-blues Blues 79
Chapter 15. Rhythm Changes 80
Chapter 16. Passages 82
The Chorus 82
Intros 83
Verses 84
Turnarounds 84
Bridge 85
Endings 87
Chapter 17. Substitutions 92
The Blues Redux 93
Tri-tone Substitution 94
Flatted 5th Descent 96
Alternative Reharmonizations 96
PART V The Charts 98
Chapter 18. Chord Charts 99
Title 100
Staves 100
Clef Sign 101
Key Signature 101
Time Signature 101
Measures 102
Tempo 102
Chapter 19. Rhythmic Notation 103
Chapter 20. Big Band Charts 106
What Does the Leader Want? 106
A Chart to Study 108

    Rehearsal Numbers..108
    Navigation...109
    Interpretation..111
    A Walk Through the Chart...116
PART VI Playing...117
Chapter 21. Comping Rhythms and Fills..118
    Rhythmic Patterns..119
    Fills...119
    Repetitious Comping..120
Chapter 22. Improvisation...121
    Listen to the Improvisers..122
    Try to Improvise...122
    Hum Your Improvisation..123
    Match Notes and Chords..123
    Playing Outside..123
    Blue Notes..124
    Arpeggios and Scales...124
    Licks...125
    Quotes..125
    Impromptu Composition..126
    Transcriptions..127
    Reward and Punishment..127
Chapter 23. Practicing..128
Appendix A: Chords...134
    Basic Chords, Chapter 4..135
    Colorful Dominant 7 and Minor 7 Chords, Chapter 5...136
    Colorful Major and Minor Chords, Chapter 6...137
    Colorful Major and Minor Chords, Chapter 6 (continued)..138
    Colorful Major and Minor Chords, Chapter 6 (continued)..139
    Diminished Chords, Chapter 7..140
    Augmented Chords, Chapter 8..141
    Suspended Chords, Chapter 8...142
    Altered 9th Interval Chords, Chapter 9...143
    Altered 5th Interval Chords, Chapter 9...144
Appendix B: Got Software?...145
    Band-in-a-Box...146
Appendix C: Jazz Jargon...148

Acknowledgments

Thanks to Callie Cotterell of PGMusic.com, makers of Band-in-a-Box® for providing a copy of their wonderful program to assist me in the making of this book and to Dan Sigmon for his comments on the book's contents.

Warm thanks to Gene Steinbach, Jerry Cozzi, and John Eaton, my teachers and musical mentors for their encouragement and influence. Gene and Jerry are gone now and sorely missed. John is still with us and playing.

*teach yourself...*Jazz Piano Comping

teach yourself... Jazz Piano Comping guides you as you learn basic accompaniment chording.

This book is for entry-level and experienced pianists who want to move into the realm of jazz and standards accompaniment and big band playing.

With the knowledge you learn in this book and a disciplined regimen of practice, you will be equipped with skills and tools that not only allow you to sit in at informal jam sessions but to expand your experience into the more advanced realms of piano accompaniments.

Books by Al Stevens

teach yourself... Rhythm Jazz Guitar

teach yourself... C++ 7th Edition

Diabetics Behaving Badly

On the Street Where You Die (Stanley Bentworth mysteries: Book 1)

A Dead Ringer (Stanley Bentworth mysteries: Book 2)

Clueless (Stanley Bentworth mysteries: Book 3)

The Rat Squad (Stanley Bentworth mysteries: Book 4)

White Collar Murders (Stanley Bentworth mysteries: Book 5)

Fugitive Warrant (Stanley Bentworth mysteries: Book 6)

Hooker Stalker Killer Pimp (Stanley Bentworth mysteries: Book 7)

Murder in the Bermuda Triangle (Stanley Bentworth mysteries: Book 8)

Assisted Homicide (Stanley Bentworth mysteries: Book 9)

Corpsicles' Cremains (Stanley Bentworth mysteries: Book 10)

Annie Somewhere

The Shadow on the Grassy Knoll

Off the Wall Stories

Golden Eagle's Final Flight (with Ron Skipper)

Ventriloquism: Art, Craft, Profession

Politically Incorrect Scripts for Comedy Ventriloquists

Welcome to Programming

...and more computer programming and usage books.

Preface

For years I've thought about writing this book but I kept putting it off, wondering if there would even be a market for it. But then, not long ago, I read in piano-based Internet discussion groups that the subject of piano accompaniment, "comping," as we call it, is mostly neglected in the literature, and yet there is a demand for it. So, retired and with time to spare, I got up from the piano bench, sat myself at the computer, and began to hammer out what I hope is a pragmatic approach to learning how to comp on the piano.

Undertaking such a project is fraught with unknowns. First, when I set about to encode my knowledge and experience about music theory, I was surprised by how much I did not know, not about how to play but about what everything is called in formal terms. Translating pragmatic practice into written form requires accuracy you don't need when you're playing. I spent a lot of time doing research to get right some things I thought I already knew. And I learned in the process.

Then, when I was well into definitions and descriptions of musical theory and harmony, I was surprised again, but this time at how much I *did* know, more to the point, how much there was to tell, how big the narrative would become.

The challenge became: how much can I leave out and still get the job done? I'm not sure I met that challenge.

You see, I wanted to condense all those ponderous, mind-boggling details into a few, readily understood words and procedures that the typical pianist could learn, remember, and put into practice. But as my work progressed, each new concept involved more muck and mire than I'd planned for. And to leave some of it out might tell only part of the story.

So, if during your studies, you find yourself buried in the minutia of notes, intervals, chords, scales, and I don't know what-all, you might come to think it not worth the effort.

However, if your goals are to be able to do what this book teaches, it is indeed worth the effort. Being able to play piano and accompany other musicians, by virtue of your repertoire and vocabulary accumulated over the years, will keep you working. I learned the hard way. With luck it won't be as hard for you, given that somehow I got enough of it written to arm you with the knowledge you need.

PART I Introduction

Welcome to *teach yourself... Jazz Piano Comping,* a guide with which you teach yourself basic jazz chording on piano for vocal and instrumental accompaniments.

The word *comp,* as used in most post-classical musical lexicons, is shorthand for *accompany.* When you comp, you accompany a singer, player, or ensemble that carries the melody or improvisation of the tune being played with your accompaniment in the background.

The nature of your accompaniment depends on the tune, the genre, and the preferences of the musician(s) being accompanied. This book teaches fundamental comping as it is played in traditional and mainstream jazz, big band music, and with the old standards.

This is Part I, and it gets you started with a touch of jazz piano background and what I think you need in order to proceed with these lessons. It's the usual who are you, who am I, and what this book is about, filler that every how-to book includes.

Chapter 1. Getting Started

We'll begin by addressing you, what you need, what you should expect to learn from this book, and who I am and why I'm qualified to teach you to be a jazz comping pianist.

Who are You?

You're a piano player who wants to play accompaniments to jazz tunes and standards from the "Great American Songbook." Perhaps you play or would like to play in a big band.

What do You Need?

Obviously you need a piano or keyboard. But you also need to bring a few other things to the project.

Reading Skills

You should be able to read two-clef piano notation to get the full benefit of these lessons. Short of showing pictures of hands on a keyboard, there is no better way to depict the voicings you'll play that make the difference between the typical left hand triad player and the accomplished piano accompanist. You don't need to be able to sight-read piano charts in real time and you won't learn that from this book. You will, however, learn to read chord symbols and rhythmic patterns. For now, you just need to know which notes on the staves correspond to which keys on the keyboard.

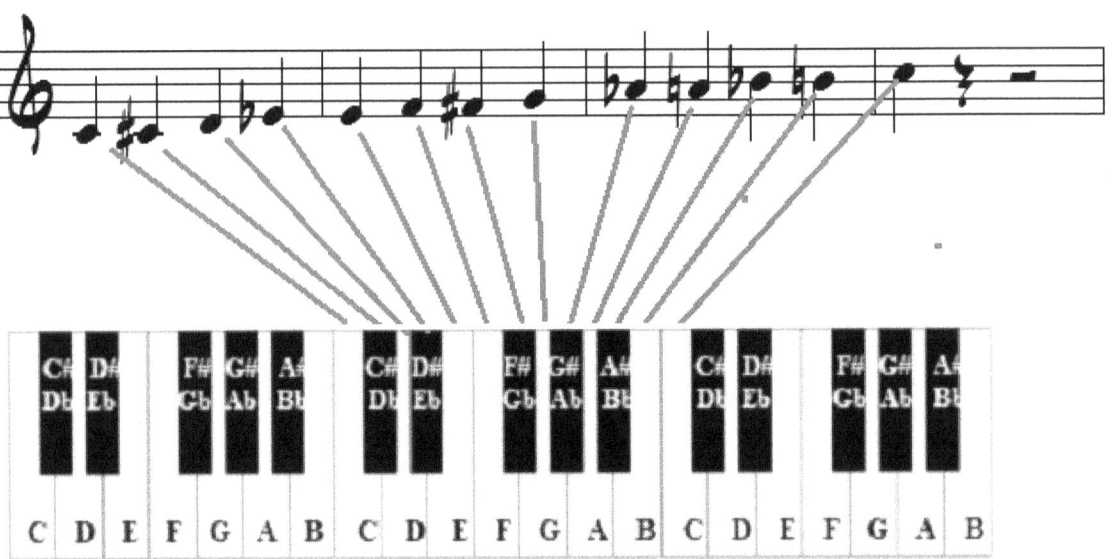

This picture is, of course, an octave on staff notation and three octaves on the keyboard. I expect you to know what this picture depicts and to know what the notated note is when you look at the keyboard and what key a note is on the keyboard when you look at the notation.

Can you read this? No? Then you might as well stop now. This is how I show you which notes to play for the chords I teach. Some people play by ear only and cannot read music. But without knowing how to read music there's no convenient way for me to depict how to play your chords. Find yourself a book with entry level piano lessons and maybe engage a teacher.

As an accompanist, you won't always have charts with the notes spelled out like the above example. That's what you expect to see on sheet music, but not often in fake books, lead sheets, or big band charts. If your goal is to play in big bands or smaller bands that use arranged charts, you must know how to read their piano charts. Following is an example. Part V explains how to do that.

First you need to learn the chords and how to play them in a comping style.

Computer Skills

To use the software I recommend, you'll need to be able to find your way around your computer's file system, and the menus and toolbars of the typical application.

Software

Unless you plan to learn at the piano only, which many students over the centuries have done, you'll need software to support these lessons. Which software you use will depend on your computer. Appendix B discusses the programs I recommend and shows some of the procedures that I use them for.

Goals

As an aspiring comping piano player, you typically wish to play jazz or old standards and accompany singers (yourself, perhaps) and/or other instrument players. If you have lofty goals— to play like Art Tatum or Oscar Peterson, for example—good for you. This book does not come close to showing the way, but it can be your first step.

Dedication, Drive and Motivation

Finally, to become a proficient comping pianist, you must have the time and desire to learn. You must be motivated and willing to practice.

Of course, anything worth doing well requires effort. There are challenges. With practice you can get past them, and if you work at it, eventually you'll be playing along with the pros.

That notwithstanding, don't give up your life to this dream unless playing piano is all that matters to you. Don't forsake your family, your day job if you have one, your health, or your community. Don't obsess.

However, if you are compelled to play music, you will play music because you can't *not* play music.

What's in this Book?

Check out this list. These are what you can expect to learn from the lessons and exercises here.

- You will learn a basic repertoire of chord changes as they are used in jazz and standards in the original keys in which most players play.

- You will learn to translate cryptic chord symbols on sheet music, lead sheets, and big band charts into keyboard chord voicings for accompaniment.

- You will learn basic music theory, enough to play piano in a jazz environment. Unlike many works on jazz chords, this one does not simply provide chord symbols and notation so you can look the chords up when you encounter them on charts. I try to explain *why* the chords sound right in a tune where you play them.

- You will learn rhythmic patterns to apply while comping, when to lay out (rest, remain tacit), when to fill, and how to enhance the performance of the musician(s) you are accompanying.

Because of my background, examples in this book draw upon old standard tunes, many of which are a part of the jazz literature. Jazz musicians have adopted the compositions of Gershwin, Porter, Rogers, and the many tin pan alley composers. You can listen to renditions of their work on YouTube, and you can download backing tracks and chord chart PDFs to support your practice of such tunes from:

http://www.alstevens.com/jazzpianocomping

Reading Musical Notation

Writing a book of prose and pictures that teaches something audible is difficult to say the least. Learning from such a book can be a challenge. Ideally, you would augment these visual lessons with one-on-one instruction from a human teacher. I don't know if that's possible for you or even whether you want to do it so I've tried to make this book stand alone as a way for you to teach yourself comping on the piano. Self-teaching is sometimes the only way. There might not be a piano teacher in your town who teaches this subject. Consequently, you will learn to play chords from these lessons by reading standard two-clef notation.

This book presents a lot of chords for you to learn. Most of the chords in the lessons use the note C as the root note (Chapter 3). That's an arbitrary choice based on these factors:

- C is probably the first note you learned when you took your first piano lesson
- The C scale is all white keys on the keyboard and *natural* notes on the notation, which makes it easier to use as a root to portray chords. The chord notation doesn't need as many *accidentals*, which are sharp, flat and natural symbols that change how you play the adjacent note.
- Chords with a C root tend to fit into the two-clef notation described below without needing ledger lines above and below the staves
- There are twelve possible roots and over twenty different kinds of chords. Explaining them all would make this book huge and repetitive

When we get into theory and chord changes (Parts III and IV), we will, of course, use many more of the roots in our chords. Until then, you should learn the chords in C and transpose them to other roots or refer to Appendix A for chord listings when you need something other than a C chord.

Chord Voicings

Voicing a chord is more than just knowing the notes and playing them all. Most beginning piano players who want to play by ear start by playing the full chord with the left hand and the melody or improvisation with the right. That might get you by, but it's not the best way to do it and it's certainly not how to get on the A list of musicians looking for piano players.

The voicings you see here are typical of what this book teaches. One or two of the notes are played by the left hand and others by the right. Most times, the two hands collaborate to provide the chord's notes in a balanced voicing that is pleasing to the listener's ear and complementary to the playing or singing of the musician(s) you are accompanying.

Such musical notation teaches you how to voice chords and chord changes, and to identify them from their names—chord symbols (Chapter 3).

The chords shown above include the root note (Chapter 3) as the lowest note played. This is called playing a chord in its *root position*. You do not always voice chords that way, however, and Chapter 10 discusses *rootless chords*.

Chord Charts

You will learn how to play music that accompanies the performance of tunes by using chord charts that depict when to play each chord and what chord to play based on its symbol and its placement on the chart. Here's an example of a tune as shown on a chord chart (Chapter 18).

Those cryptic letters and numbers—G7, C7, etc.—above the staves are *chord symbols* (Chapter 3), the names of the chords. The slashes on the staves indicate the measure's beats, and which beat each chord is to be played on. By the time you complete these lessons, you will have learned several ways to play each chord on the chart and you will play tunes by selecting from those ways based on the chord symbols and your hand positions on the keyboard. If that looks hard, don't worry. It all comes clear as you progress through the lessons.

The Changes

We discuss *chord progressions* and *chord sequences*. They are the same thing, meaning a set of chords played one after the other to achieve a harmonic objective. Musicians typically call these sets *chord changes* or, simply, *changes*. We'll tend to use this idiom because that's what you'll hear on the bandstand.

Accompaniment

Accompaniment is playing background music to accompany a singer, solo instrument, combo, or even a complete band. *Comping* is, for this discussion, playing accompanying chords and fills not necessarily in strict four beat or whatever the time signature is, but with player-chosen rhythmic patterns.

There are other rhythmic time and tempo styles that you must eventually learn, such as waltzes and Latin rhythms, but they should come natural to you after you've completed these lessons and gotten some playing experience. For now, we'll stick to swinging four-beat and ballads with the occasional 3/4 tune tossed in.

Keyboard Span

For these lessons, we'll keep the chord voicings within about three octaves at the approximate center of the eighty-eight. In other words, we'll stay mostly within the range of the treble and bass clef staves.

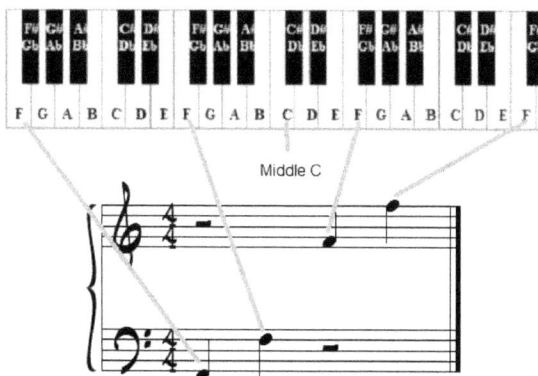

That makes it easier for the book to depict and for you to read and play the chords. Later, you can move what you've learned up and down the keyboard as your impromptu accompaniment skills evolve. Occasionally, we might use a note or two outside this range, but you won't see any *8va* symbols or stacks of ledger lines above and below the staves, and you won't be asked to play hand stretches that are beyond the reach of a small pair of adult human hands. No left hand tenths, for example.

The limited range, which we use for learning, is far from absolute. You wouldn't want to play Count Basie's piano part by staying within the three middle octaves.

Who am I?

I'm a retired professional musician and writer with about 60 years of playing gigs ranging from piano bars to concert halls, night clubs to weddings, private parties to international jazz festivals, cruise ships, and even the occasional outdoor strawberry and frog legs festival.

I play several instruments at performance levels. Not a virtuoso mind you, but a competent sideman. My musical education (self-taught) began with ragtime piano when I was a boy and progressed through Dixieland on several instruments, be-bop, progressive and mainstream jazz, show tunes, and cocktail music.

I've performed and recorded with many jazz greats, among them Al Hirt, Wild Bill Davison, Bud Freeman, Billy Butterfield, Louis Bellson, Buddy Morrow, and other old dead guys. I've played in the *ghost bands* of Tommy Dorsey, Harry James, and Benny Goodman. I've accompanied vocalists such as Connie Haines, Joni James, and Nancy Kelly. I was pianist with the Bill Allred Classic Jazz Band for five years and played in the Rosie O'Grady's Good Time Jazz Band in Orlando off and on for several years. I was, for many years, a sideman with countless Dixieland bands and combos in the Washington, DC area and on Florida's Space Coast. I have been a member of the American Federation of Musicians, Orlando Local 389 since the 1960s. I'm now a life member of that local.

Oh, yeah. I sing too. Not very well, but good enough for the saloons. Much of my accompaniment chops were grown in piano bars where it was just me and sit-in singers. When you accompany yourself and tipping customers, you want to do it right, to make the crooner or canary sound good.

All that self-aggrandizing puffery aside, times have changed. In my day, a pianist walked onto a gig, sat at the piano, and began playing. When venues stopped having pianos, pianists were expected to bring electronic keyboards and amplifiers, and I got too old to schlep all that heavy stuff, so I put in for retirement.

Why the Piano?

The piano is a standalone instrument for solos and accompaniments. You don't need a rhythm section. The instrument supports everything: melody, chords, and rhythm. And for some reason, virtually every musician and vocalist wants to play the piano. Some do. Wynton Marsalis, Arturo Sandoval, Harry Connick, Jr., Gerry Mulligan, Nat Cole, and Sarah Vaughn can (or could) hold their own at the piano with any band.

Jazz

This book is mostly about playing jazz accompaniments, but the principles taught here apply to many other kinds of musical accompaniment. So let's take a look at jazz itself and how it has influenced the styles of music you will accompany on the piano.

Jazz Bands

A jazz band is an ensemble of musicians that play jazz music. Here's a picture of the "Original Dixieland Jazz Band," a group of white musicians who capitalized on the growing popularity of African-American jazz music in the 1920s and recorded the first commercially successful jazz recording.

teach yourself...Jazz Piano Comping

The term "jazz band" now refers to many kinds of groups. What we used to call "dance bands" and "big bands" are now called "jazz bands," even when few of their arrangements involve improvisation (Chapter 22) and few of their musicians have improvising skills. For our purposes, any ensemble that includes a pianist accompanying other musicians is a combo or a big band.

Jazz Piano

Jazz played on piano is as old as jazz music itself. Its roots are in *ragtime*, a syncopated style of piano playing that emulates marches, and *blues*, a form of vocal and primitive instrument music with common chord changes (Chapter 14) and that were originally known as *field* songs because field workers sang the songs while they worked. Ragtime evolved into the so-called "stride" piano styling of the 1920s when the piano was typically the only instrument being played at rent parties, in saloons, and in the parlors of bordellos. The blues morphed into the "boogie-woogie" style of solo piano that emphasizes eight-to-the-bar left hand bass note patterns.

Piano became an integral component of jazz bands in the legendary hands of performers such as Jelly Roll Morton, Duke Ellington, Count Basie, Earl Fatha Hines, and Fats Waller.

Prominent soloists and players in small ensembles were Willie the Lion Smith, Nat King Cole, and Clarence Pinetop Smith.

Apparently you needed a nickname to be a successful pianist in those days.

Jazz Pianists

There are many great jazz pianists, pioneers now gone from us, and you can find their recordings online. Among them, in no particular order, are Thelonious Monk, Art Tatum, Bud Powell, Oscar Peterson, Bill Evans, George Shearing, Dave McKenna, Billy Taylor, Dave Brubeck, Erroll Garner, Mary Lou Williams, Teddy Wilson, Marian McPartland, Ahmad Jamal, Hazel Scott, Wynton Kelly, and many others.

Those players are gone but they have many extant successors, great jazz pianists who inspire and influence our playing, among them, Chick Corea, Monty Alexander, Diana Krall, Dick Hyman, Herbie Hancock, Keith Jarrett, Marcus Roberts, and so on.

Those are only a few of the famous ones, known for their solo work and performances with small combos that feature the piano as the lead instrument.

The players that interest us, however, are often the ones nobody ever hears about because they sit quietly at the piano backing up the prominent vocalists and instrumentalists, often never playing a solo, usually cropped from the album cover pictures, and in high demand by the players and singers who want the best in piano accompaniment.

Some of these pianists are and were: Alan Broadbent, Ray Sherman, Gene Schroeder, John Eaton, Eddie Costa, Ralph Sharon, Mel Powell, Jess Stacy, and many others. Never heard of them? That's not surprising. Their roles in musical ensembles were to accompany front line performers, to back up solo artists, and to make everybody else sound good. Many of them had separate careers playing in trios and solo performances, but they did not achieve the fame bestowed upon the Garners, Tatums and Petersons. They are, however, the ones to listen to as you learn to play jazz piano accompaniments.

Why Jazz?

Why indeed? Why do musicians want to play jazz? Except for a few well-known performers, there's not much money being made playing jazz. There aren't many paying gigs, maybe because so many amateur musicians are so eager to play jazz that they take gigs for low pay or sit in for nothing. Club owners have become accustomed to paying from zero to squat for talent, and disk jockeys and karaoke operators have bumped live music into something from the past.

We jazz musicians are our own worst enemies and our own biggest fans. So why the enthusiasm among musicians to play jazz?

To the dedicated, motivated player, jazz is a calling, a passion, a need to stretch one's creativity beyond the printed page of notation to play what we hear, by ear, either alone or in collaboration with other jazz musicians.

And jazz music itself is compelling in ways that are difficult if not impossible to describe. When you hear it, you'll know. When you play it, you'll be hooked.

Jazz and Standards

We discuss the playing of *jazz* and *standard* tunes. That would seem to be a clear distinction, but there is a lot of overlap. Jazz tunes consist of pieces written usually by jazz musicians specifically for jazz performances. Often they don't have lyrics. Examples are *Joy Spring, Oleo, Blue Bossa,* and *Take Five*. Standard tunes, on the other hand, are tunes from the so-called "Great American Songbook" and they include show tunes, tin pan alley, and some contemporary pop tunes. Many of them have been assimilated into the jazz repertoire and have become *de facto* jazz standards. Examples are *Stardust, There Will Never Be Another You, Just the Way You Are,* and virtually any tune written by Duke Ellington.

Exercises and Practicing

These lessons include exercises interspersed among the explanations of chords and theory. Included among them are charts of tunes with which you can practice what you've learned. I encourage you not to skip over these exercises. The best way to learn the inner concepts of playing music is to play those concepts, and the best way to do that is to apply them in the contexts in which you will use them in your playing. In other words, by playing tunes. Chapter 23 addresses these ideas in more detail. For now, perform the exercises and play the tunes as they are presented.

PART II Scales and Chords

The foundation of piano comping is found in the chords you play as accompaniment to the rest of the musical entourage whether that be you as a solo vocalist, in a duo, a combo, or a big band. To understand chords beyond just how to play a few of them is to understand their underpinning scales and the tones and intervals that make them up.

Don't worry. I'm not trying to get you to practice scales endlessly like your teacher might. That's not the object here. But I want you to understand them, so you can learn the chords with an informed approach.

You'll see a lot here in Part II and other parts of this book that teach concepts from the view of the beloved key of C. That's done on purpose. Otherwise the book would be twelve times as big.

But remember, when you know all about the key of C, then you know all about eleven other keys, their scales and their chords. But you might not know that you know it. It's just a matter of having your hands fall where they need to be as you play piano accompaniments.

Chapter 2. Tones, Intervals and Scales

To prepare to learn musical theory (Part III), we must first understand tones, intervals and scales. A complete understanding of any one of these three requires some understanding of the other two.

How do they fit together? A *scale* is a series of eight *intervals*, each of which is a pair of *notes*. A *tone* is a pair of notes two notes apart. A *half-tone* is a pair of adjacent notes. Got that? If not, you will soon.

Tones

Scales are constructed of *tones*, and we'll see how. For now, know that a tone is two notes that are, on the keyboard, two keys apart. A half-tone is, therefore two adjacent keys. By adjacent, we mean, as you might expect, next to one another. But although the keyboard makes it seem that C and D, for example, are adjacent, since their sides abut one another, they aren't adjacent with respect to tones. The black key that is C♯ / D♭ is between them. So, C and D are a tone. But C and C♯ are a half tone, also called a *semitone*. So are E and F because there is no black key between them. The keys that are C♯ and E♭ are, however, a tone because the white key D is between them.

Here the relationship between tones and half tones is shown on the keyboard:

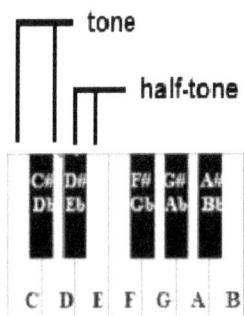

And here it is in notation:

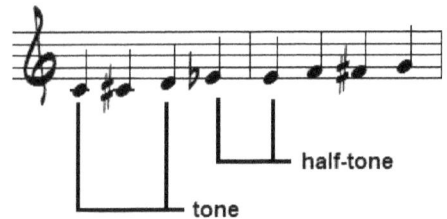

Actually, every black key is a flat *and* a sharp as the keyboard picture above shows, and some white keys are also flats or sharps. B is C♭, C is B♯, E is F♭, and F is E♯. Confused? Don't worry. You rarely encounter these note names in your reading experiences unless you're playing classical music, in which case you're already way past this discussion.

Intervals

An *interval* is the distance between two notes in a scale and, as you will learn in Chapter 3, in a chord. Here is the C major scale but with the interval numbers added.

The ordinal numbers under the notes are intervals. In the C scale, D is the 2nd interval, E the 3rd, and so on.

When we get into the discussion of chords in the remaining chapters of Part II we'll go as high as the 13th interval, which, in the C scale, would be A above the treble clef. An interval number is relative to a major scale's tonic note, which is C in the above example.

The 1st interval is also called the *tonic*.

The Octave

An *octave* is an interval comprised of two notes that span eight notes in a scale, thus its name, but it really spans twelve half tones. So, for example, C at one ledger line below the treble clef and C in the third space comprise an octave like this:

Here are more octaves:

The two notes in an octave can use any of the notes in the chromatic scale explained soon.

Scales

Students of musical instruments are encouraged to practice *scales* repetitively until they can play them by memory. But some teachers never explain why you should practice scales other than to say that scales improve your technique. That's true, of course, but there are other reasons to know scales when you improvise (Chapter 22). For now, an understanding of scales and the relationships between their notes is essential to a full understanding of music theory.

Here's the C scale.

You'll be seeing a lot of this scale in these lessons. It's our foundation.

I know I'm hammering you with scale information, but fear not, you don't have to practice scales for these lessons. It wouldn't hurt you to do so, but it isn't mandatory. You need to understand scales and know the notes that comprise them, but you don't have to play them proficiently. Music teachers across the land are hurling their metronomes at me right now, but I hold my ground. To play proficient chordal accompaniment on the piano, you do not need to have developed a proficiency with scales. Improvisation (Chapter 22), however, is a different matter.

Chromatic Scale

Keyboard notes played in succession—when you play the next key adjacent to the current one—are also the *chromatic* scale beginning on whichever note you started with and ending wherever you wish.

You just learned that adjacent notes are a *half tone* away from each other. There are twelve half-tone notes in an *octave*, and if you play them in succession in either direction, up or down, you are playing what is called the *chromatic* scale.

And, no matter where you start playing an ascending chromatic scale the note immediately after the twelfth note, the thirteenth note, of course, is an *octave* above the first one.

Major Scales

A scale is a series of notes with intervals measured in whole and half tones. Consider again the C major scale.

It's almost the alphabet except that it begins on C and jumps back to A after the G. But remember the intervals. C is the 1st interval, D is the 2nd, and so on. That's why when musicians refer to the 4th in the C scale, for example, they are referring to the note F. It's the 4th interval in the scale.

Intervals are crucial to an understanding of harmonic theory. This is why you need to understand scales. When you hear mention of the 3rd, 5th, 7th, whatever, you need to know which note that is in the current chord under discussion. In a C major chord, the 3rd is E. In E♭, the 3rd is G, in F, the 3rd is A, and so on.

To the uninitiated, the notes in a major scale are just letters. But think of the tune we all learned from *The Sound of Music*, which uses other names for the notes in a major scale.

"Do, re, mi, fa, sol, la, ti, do."

These names, called collectively, *solfeggio,* can apply to any major scale. It just depends on which note you begin and end with. If you are in the key of C, *do* at the beginning is C, and *do* at the end is C an octave above the first one.

If that seems too simple, it isn't. The C to B scale consists of all white key notes, which is obvious on the keyboard. Consider the E♭ major scale:

Some of these notes, the first one included, are flatted notes.

The first note in the scale is called the *tonic*. From there, a major scale moves upward in tonal intervals like this:

Tonic, whole step, whole step, half step, whole step, whole step, whole step, half step.

That last half step lands on the tonic note an octave higher than the original.

In theoretical jargon, the 4th interval is the *subdominant*, and the 5th interval is the *dominant*.

Minor Scales

The C *minor* scale is formed with these intervals:

This is the C *natural* minor scale. There are also *harmonic* and *melodic* minor scales. Don't worry about them.

Summary of Scales

There's more to scales than this chapter describes, but it's enough for a general discussion of theory.

I will, however, ease your apprehension about putting to memory all the notes in all the scales. Instead of remembering the component notes of, for example, the minor chord of a specified tonic, you will learn how to play that chord. If the music sheet says, for example, E♭7, you will know how to form that chord several ways on the keyboard. That's a lot of things to remember, but more than some abstract recollection of note names and intervals is involved. With practice you will learn which chord to play because of how it sounds.

Memory is something you remember. You remember things long term that you drum into your memory repetitively. The more often you play a chord in the right place in a tune, the more deeply you burn it into your harmonic and muscle memories. *Harmonic memory* is what your mind knows a chord or sequence of chords *sound* like. *muscle memory*, in this context, is what they *feel* like with your hands on the keyboard. When the next correct chord comes to you on its own without your having to think about it, you have that chord nailed in those memories. On to the next chord.

The same thing applies to every possible sequence of chord changes. Eventually you will play all of them so often they will become second nature.

Chapter 3. Chord Basics

This discussion explains chords and how they are constructed. You probably already know some of this, but I suggest that you at least look it over to make sure we're speaking the same language.

Chords

A *chord* is two or more different notes played at the same time. When you press more than one note on the keyboard at the same time, you're playing a chord. Which chord you play depends on which keys you press.

Here is the ever-popular C chord, the first chord every student learns, the triad of notes C, E, and G.

A *triad* is a chord with three notes consisting of the root note, the 3rd and the 5th. It is the basis for virtually all the chords you learn in these lessons. There are many Cs, Es, and Gs on a piano keyboard. You can play any combination of them to make a C chord. But for accompaniments we prefer to use the closest voicings, the configuration of notes that are closest to one another and that sound good in the current musical context.

Chordal instruments—those that play more than one note at a time, such as virtually any stringed or keyboard instrument—can play chords alone. Wind and vocal ensembles combine the notes of multiple instruments each played by individual musicians to form chords.

Chord Symbols

Most piano lead sheets, sheet music and big band charts include *chord symbols* above the staff. The symbol is the chord's name, the name by which you identify it and discuss it with other musicians. Eventually, chord symbols should be all the harmonic information you need to play accompaniments from a chart.

There are variations of how chords are named, and there are chord symbols that you won't need to know to get through this book. For an exhaustive treatment of the subject, search Wikipedia for "chord names." I promise you'll come hurrying back here after you read way more than you ever wanted or needed to know.

Here are the elements of chord symbols as we know them:

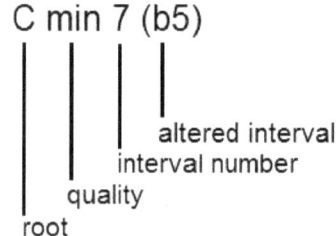

All but the root element can be omitted in the naming of a chord. Its name, however, tells you what notes to play. The example shown here contains most of the components of the chord symbols that we use. Following is a discussion of each of them.

Root

A chord symbol always begins with the name of the note that is its *root*. In the illustration, C is the root of the chord. Everything past that expands on the root. If there is only the root, the chord is assumed to be a major triad with the root note at its beginning. You'll learn more about the root later in this chapter.

Quality

The *quality* defines the chord as being major, minor, diminished, augmented, suspended, or major 7th, 9th, or 13th using these tokens:

- maj (implied so typically omitted)
- min
- dim
- aug
- sus
- Maj7
- Maj9
- Maj13

Quality Abbreviations

Some chord naming conventions abbreviate minor chords (explained later) with a lower-case 'm' instead of 'min.' That's a common practice. Some use a simple dash (-) to indicate a minor chord. Here are three ways you might see, for example, a G minor chord symbol:

- Gm
- Gmin
- G-

Augmented chords (Chapter 8) are often notated with the + symbol rather than the 'aug' suffix.

And sometimes a 5 is added.

- Gaug
- G^+
- G^{+5}

Diminished chords (Chapter 7) sometimes use a degree symbol.

- Gdim
- G^o

The half diminished chord is also called the min7($\flat$5) (Chapter 7) and can be notated with a slashed o.

- Gmin7($\flat$5)
- $G^\varnothing$

Major 7 (Chapter 6) is often encoded with a delta (Δ) symbol.

- GMaj7
- G^Δ

Interval Number

The interval number identifies a note that is not part of the chord's triad but that is included in the chord's voicing. Rather than use the added note's name, chord symbols use interval numbers relative to the scale of the root note. This number can be 2, 6, 7, 9, 11, or 13. (2 and 11 are rarely used in the styles of music we play.) You'll learn what these numbers mean as you encounter chords that employ them in the lessons that follow.

Altered Interval

An altered interval, usually but not always shown in parentheses, specifies that one of the chord's notes is to be sharped or flatted. The note is also a number interval relative to the root's major scale. For example, the ($\flat$5) altered interval specifies that the 5th of the chord, G in a C chord, is to be flatted.

The parentheses around the altered interval is intended to disambiguate what would otherwise be confusing notation. For example:

A$\flat$9 = an A$\flat$ chord with a 9th added.

A($\flat$9) = an A chord with a flatted 9th.

If there are no ambiguities, some copyists omit the parentheses. For example, B$\flat$$\sharp$11 is unambiguous without the parentheses.

Some copyists use superscripts to disambiguate the symbol like this:

A♭^{9} = an A♭ chord with the 9th interval.

A♭$^{♭9}$ = an A♭ chord with the 9th interval flatted.

These conventions can be confusing particularly when the chart is handwritten. I prefer to use the parentheses.

Standard Symbols?

You just learned that we have various ways to name chord symbols. We have no established, recognized, and accepted one way to do that. These lessons use chord symbol conventions that most musicians will recognize. But be prepared to run into all manner of alternate spellings for chord symbols.

The apparent inconsistencies in chord symbol names are a product of the evolutionary nature of musical notation. The differences came from multiple sources and musical eras, and were diversely accepted conventions by various musical cultures. They were evolving all over the place and musicians weren't always talking to one another about it. No one standard has ever taken hold or become *de facto*, and musicians have come to learn the various chord-naming idioms and to work with them. You will, too.

If you see an unfamiliar chord symbol on a chart, ask other musicians. If they don't know, agree on a chord that fits the tune based on the notes they are all playing. If it's a so-called *head chart*, just agree on something that sounds right.

Don't you wish they'd settle on one way to do it? So do I. To that end, this book uses mostly the first symbol conventions that the lists above identify. I want to keep everything on a common level to make it easier for me to explain and for you to learn. After you get out into the world and start pulling charts from folders, you'll be on your own.

The Root Note

As you learned above, every chord has a *root* note, and that note is the first element of the chord symbol, its *name*. The root note for CMaj7, for example, is C. The root note for F7 is F. And so on. To hear how a chord's root contributes to what the chord sounds like within a tune, play this simple exercise, which arpeggiates a C major chord and ends on the same chord.

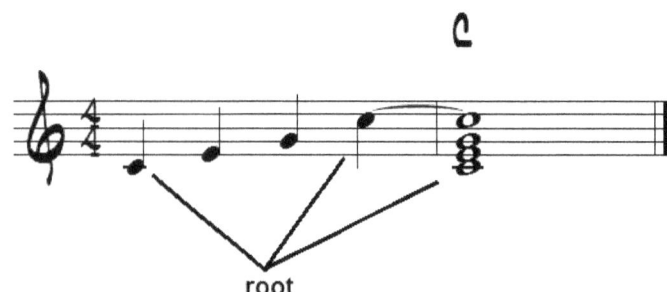

Do you hear how any note other than the top C in the second measure would not fit? At least not in this context. If you don't hear that, try it. Play notes other than the C in place of it.

C is the root note of the C chord. It sounds the chord's harmonic foundation in a way that satisfies the listener's ear. There's a lot more to it than this simple example demonstrates, and you'll learn much of that in Chapter 11.

You need to know the root so you can fit the chord into the musical passage being played. Which is why the chord symbol, the C shown above the second measure, includes its root note as the first part of its name even when the voicing might not include the root note (Chapter 10).

Inversions

The chords shown so far place the root notes on the lowest-pitched of the chord's notes on the keyboard. That is the usual way chords are thought of by pianists and other chordal instrument players. But for each triad, for example, there are three ways to play its closest grouping. The first way is called the *root position* and has the root note on the lowest note of the grouping. The other two ways are called *inversions*, which means that the lowest note played in the chord is other than the root.

The C chord's root position consists of the notes C, E, and G, beginning on the bottom. The *first* inversion is played E, G, and C, and the *second* inversion is played G, C, and E. Here is the C chord played in its root position and in both its inversions.

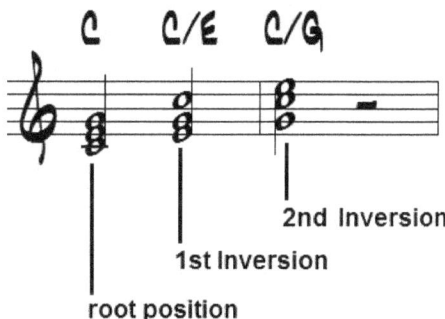

Observe the slash suffixes on two of the chord symbols. Those are explained next.

Slash Chords

When you see a chord symbol with a slash (/) and a note name, such as in the two inversions shown above, that notation of a *slash chord* specifies that the chord should be played with the slash note on the bottom at the lowest pitch. For example:

This is a C7 chord (Chapter 4). It includes the four notes that comprise a C7:

C, E, G, and B♭.

The *order* of the notes is not, however, what usually see for a C7 chord. That chord typically has C, the root, as the lowest pitched note in the chord and each next higher-pitched note as the next successive note played up the keyboard. This C7 chord has E as the lowest pitched note. It also voices the chord differently with respect to the order up the keyboard in which you play the notes. Get used to that. That's how you will learn to play chords when you comp.

This slash naming convention serves to say that a note other than the root should be the lowest-pitched note sounded when the chord is played.

There's more to slash chords than that but for now simply play the chord the way you know it. Your playing will not clash with anything that's happening in the tune or that the rest of the band is playing. If it does, you'll hear it and you can do something to fix it then.

Chapter 4. Basic Chords

We start with four basic chords, the *major*, the *minor*, the *dominant 7*, and the *minor 7*. Most of your comping will use these chords or variations of them.

In this chapter and the ones that follow, I'll show the chords with all their notes in single, treble-clef notation. That way you can easily identify which notes are in each of the chords. Then I'll show the same chord in two-clef notation so you can see how you can voice the chord with two hands while you accompany someone.

Major

A *major* chord is three notes, called a *triad*, that include the root note and the 3rd and 5th intervals (vertical distance in tones between notes in a scale, Chapter 2).

Here is the C major scale, which you need to know to understand the C major chord.

The notes are: C, D, E, F, G, A, B, and C

A C major chord includes C, the root or first note in the scale, E, the 3rd note in the scale, and G, the 5th note in the scale.

We saw this C chord in Chapter 3. We return to it as our launching platform for learning to play chordal accompaniments. Here is how you might encounter it in a chart:

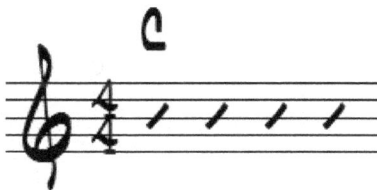

The chord symbol above the staff identifies the chord to be played at that point in the tune, in this case on the measure's downbeat (beat 1 of 4).

Here's how to play the C chord.

There are many other ways to voice and play a C chord. For now, memorize this one and use it when C is called for.

I won't show the chart every time past this, only each chord's notes and how to play the chord.

This is only the C major chord. There are eleven other major chords, one for each of the notes. So if you see an F chord, for example, you'd play it like this.

Does that make sense? The voicing is the same as the C chord, 3rd in the treble clef, 5th and root in the bass clef. Same intervals, different pitches. So now you know one way to voice two chords, C and F. You'll learn lots of ways to make all the chords as you progress with your learning.

Minor

A *minor* chord, also a triad, is almost the same as the major chord except the 3rd interval is flatted (one half tone lower).

Here's the C minor chord.

Here's how to play it.

Once again, you have many options for voicing a minor chord. Use this one for now. Don't forget about the other eleven root notes.

Dominant 7

The dominant 7 chord is a major triad that adds and flats the 7th interval in the root's scale. Back to the C major scale.

The 7th interval is B. When you lower the 7th note to the next half-tone down, in this case, B♭, you are turning the major chord into a *dominant 7th*. This chord would then be:

The notes for C7 are: C, E, G, and B♭.

Here's how you'll play the C7.

Notice the two notes in the bass clef, C and B♭, the root and the flatted 7th – which we call the *dominant 7*—of the C major scale. That voicing is called the *cup,* among other things, and you will use it a lot in comping.

Minor 7

A minor 7 chord is a minor triad with the addition of the 7th note of the scale flatted.

The notes for Cmin7 are: C, E♭, G, and B♭.

Here's how you will play the Cmin7 chord.

It's the same voicing with the cup as you used for the C7 above, but the 3rd interval, the E in the treble clef, is flatted.

Other Roots

You've just learned the four basic chords, all shown with the root note of C (and F for the major chord for a comparison). There are, of course, other notes on the chromatic scale within the spread of an octave, and each of them, when used as a chord's root note, contains the same configuration of interval notes taken from its scales.

That should imply that if you know, for example, how to play the vanilla Cmin7 chord just shown, you should also know how to play, for example, the B♭min7 chord and all the others.

They don't look the same, do they? They aren't because they don't have the same notes. But they are too because they have the same intervals relative to their respective root notes, C and B♭.

Of course, because the chords are minor 7 chords, their 7th intervals, B and A, respectively, are flatted to B♭ and A♭, respectively in the chords.

Here's how you'd play them with a cup in the bass clef and the 3rd and 5th on the treble clef.

There are ten more minor 7 chords, one for each of the other ten roots. And there are twelve of each of the other kinds of the four basic chords. I don't expect you to automatically know the notes in all of them from this simple two-chord comparison. You must practice playing them all until their fingerings become one with their names in your harmonic and muscle memories.

Of course, to put all this to memory, you need to know all twelve major scales.

Appendix A contains the voicings for all the basic chords and those discussed in later chapters. Use that Appendix not only to learn how to voice the chords but also as a reference for which notes are in which chords by name.

Exercise: Chord Practicing

Get a pack of blank 3x5 cards and a felt-tip marker. On each card write the name of a chord. Only the names, not the notes or notation for the chords. These are the cards you want. For each root: C, D♭, D, E♭, F, F#, G, A♭, A, B♭, and B, write the name of one kind of chord on its own card. These are the chord types: major, minor, dominant 7 and minor 7. Use the chord symbols we've discussed so far. That's 48 cards to make. This will be your practice deck and your memory-stimulation deck. We'll just call it your *chord deck*.

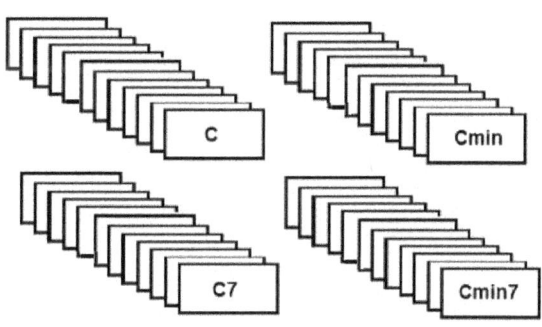

You learned the voicings of the C chords in this chapter. You have not, however, learned how to voice chords with roots other than C. So, open Appendix A where you can find those voicings. Look at that reference only when you have to. It is better to use your knowledge of the intervals of each of the chord types to transpose to the next chord you want to play.

1. Shuffle all 48 cards into what is now the random-order chord deck.
2. Place the deck face up where you can see and reach it as you sit at your piano.
3. Play on the piano the chord named on the topmost card. If you don't remember its voicing and cannot figure out how to transpose to it from what you already learned, refer to Appendix A.
4. Play the chord several times, always looking at and thinking of the chord symbol on the card.
5. Put that card aside.
6. Play the next chord.
7. Continue playing chords and turning cards until you've played them all.

Repeat this exercise until you can play any of these 48 chords by name without thinking about it.

The point of this practice is to drill into your brain and muscle memory what each chord sounds like to your ears and feels like in your hands and to associate those sounds and feelings with each chord's symbol/name.

Your objective is to be able to see the symbol and play the chord without having to think about it. Those symbols are what you see on lead sheets, in fake books, and on big band charts. You must be able to play the correct chords in real time as the rest of the ensemble plays the tune.

There are many more chords coming in the chapters that follow and you'll add cards to the chord deck as you go along.

You'll be happy to know that the majority of your accompaniments will employ the four chord types you learned in this chapter. That's right, four types, twelve roots each, a total of 48 chords to memorize.

Does it sound like a lot? Well, it is, but remember, each chord type, each major chord, for example, is formed from the root, and they all follow the same structural voicing relative to the root.

Practice: Your First Tune

Next, you should put what you've learned into practice, not just playing the chords as you did with the deck of chords, but by playing them in the context of a real tune, one that you might find yourself playing on a gig somewhere.

This tune was published in 1902 and written by Hughie Cannon. Its chord changes are found in many other standard and jazz tunes. This chart is a simple accompaniment. You won't always be playing the same chord voicing for each chord and you won't always be playing whole and half notes during accompaniments. This tune and others like it in the lessons that follow are intended to drill the chords you've learned into your harmonic and muscle memories. Later, you'll move on to more sophisticated voicings and rhythmic patterns. You'll also learn more sophisticated chord changes for tunes such as this one.

Chapter 5. Colorful Dominant 7 and Minor 7 Chords

You learned about dominant and minor 7 chords in Chapter 4. Chapter 11 will explain how those chords are used to harmonically resolve to other chords in your vocabulary. Now you'll learn about dominant and minor 7 chords that use intervals above 7 to add "color" to their sound, make them more pleasing to listeners, and, in some cases, reflect an altered tone in the tune's melody.

9 Chord

A 9 chord is a dominant 7 with a 9th interval voiced above the 7th like these chords, which are C9 and Cmin9:

A 9 chord has dominant 7 and 9 intervals, so C9 includes not only a B♭ (the dominant 7th) but a D (the 9th) as well.

Here's how to play the 9 and min9 chords.

A bebop pianist once told me that if I wanted a "modern" sound on piano, I should add a 9th to every chord where it wouldn't clash and that I would learn what does clash with experimenting. I tried it and it seemed to work.

13 Chord

A 13 chord is a dominant 7 with the 13th interval added like this:

That's the simple explanation and it's probably all you need to know. When the chart tells you to play a 13 chord, choose from the intervals presented above: 1, 3, 5, dominant 7, and 13.

Here's how you'd play the 13 chords.

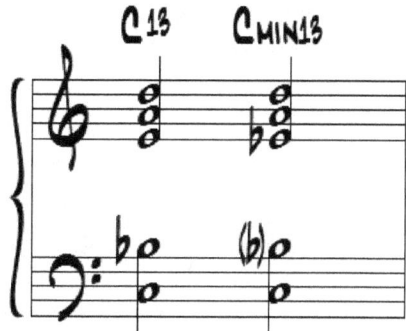

Those are the only notes you need to include and sometimes you don't need to include all of them. But why the D, the 9th? Because it fits within the formal definition of a 13 chord and it sounds nice.

And why not G, the 5th? Because you don't need it. Try it. Play those two voicings and include the G above middle C. It's there and you can hear it but it doesn't add anything.

Before the chord police come careening out swinging their batons, let me say that what you just learned is all you need to know about the notes in the 13 chord.

However, here's the formal rule:

Whenever you see a chord symbol with an odd interval greater than 7, such as 9, 11, or 13, the notes that are part of the formal chord include the dominant 7 along with the other odd intervals between 7 and up to and including the odd interval named in the chord symbol.

So, a 9 chord includes the dominant 7 and the 9th intervals, and that's what you learned a few paragraphs up.

The 13 is different. The C13, for example, includes the 13th interval, which is an A in this case. The 13th interval also implies the presence of the 9th, D in a C13, and the dominant 7, B♭ in this case.

The 13 chord also implies the inclusion of the 11th interval, F in a C13, but it is rarely played.

To repeat ourselves and hammer it home, the 13 chord includes the dominant 7, the 9, the 11, and the 13. Confused? Me too. Look at it this way. Starting from the top: the 13 includes the 11.

That implied 11 includes the 9. The implied 9 includes the dominant 7. Better? I didn't think so. Here's a formal C 13 chord.

Do you really want to play all those notes just to be correct? Me neither.

You may omit any or all of the higher odd intervals, keeping the dominant 7, and the chord will fit harmonically. It might not be as pretty but it will fit.

A C7, for example, works whenever the arrangement calls for a C9 or a C13. You won't be playing the full chord, but what you do play fits harmonically and doesn't create any dissonance.

Why would you do that? You're hammering away in a rehearsal or performance. Your eye sees that F♯13 chord. You don't remember how to play it or you haven't learned it yet. So you play the F♯7 because anything with an odd interval number works with only the dominant 7. You look around. Nobody is glaring at you. You got away with it. If you're like me, you'll do such things all your musical life.

The F♯7 works because the higher numbers imply the presence of a dominant 7, and the other odd intervals are harmonic excess.

Exercise: More Chord Practicing

Now you'll add to the chord deck you started in Chapter 4 by adding the 9 and 13 chords you just learned.

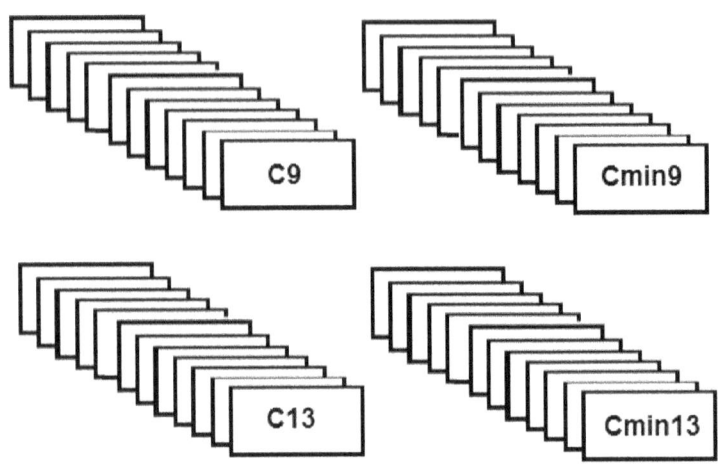

These are the cards you want. For each root: C, D♭, D, E♭, F, F♯, G, A♭, A, B♭, and B, write the name of one kind of chord on its own card, this time only the 9 and 13 chords. That's 48 cards to add to the deck.

You learned the voicings of the 9 and 13 chords in this chapter. You have not, however, learned how to voice the chords with roots other than C. So open Appendix A where you can find those voicings. Look at that reference only when you have to. It is better to use your knowledge of the intervals of each of the chord types to transpose to the next chord you want to play.

1. Shuffle these 48 cards into the chord deck you've been building since Chapter 4.
2. Repeat the practice regimen you learned in Chapter 4 except now use the cards from both chapters.

Repeat this exercise until you can play any of these chords by name without thinking about it.

There are more chords to come and you'll add cards to the deck as you go along.

Chapter 6. Colorful Major and Minor Chords

You learned the basic major and minor triads and their dominant 7 intervals in Chapter 4. Those chords, when played, fit harmonically wherever the chart specifically names them. But they have that bland vanilla sound. Below are chords you can play not only when their names are given on a chart but usually when only the basic major or minor chord is called for without a dominant 7th or colorful intervals.

Maj7

The Maj7 chord is the staple for playing a nice "colorful" sound where a major or minor chord is called for. You often see it spelled out at the end of an arrangement when the (natural) 7th interval is the final melody note or is within the ending chord's harmony. You form a Maj7 or min(Maj7) chord by adding the 7th interval to the triad. Charts often call the chord symbol out specifically.

Here's how to play these chords.

The min(Maj7) chord is not as widely used as is the Maj7. I know of one tune, *Maybe September*, that begins with it because the tune is in a minor key and the first phrase of the melody includes the tonic key's major 7th interval.

You should avoid substituting one of these for simple major or minor chords when the melody note is the chord's root and is sung or played in a register close to the 7th interval.

Maj9

The Maj9 chord is a Major 7 chord with a 9th interval added. For a root of C this addition would be a D.

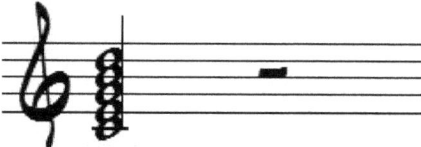

Here is how you would voice the C Maj9 chord.

This chord essentially adds color to the Major 7 chord to give it a more pleasing sound. You usually see it on a chart when an instrument ensemble includes its added notes.

Maj13

The Maj13 chord is a Major 9 chord with a 13th interval added. For a root of C this addition would be an A.

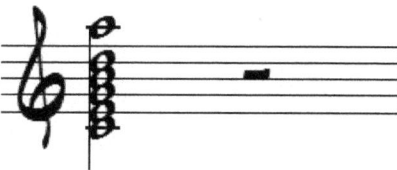

Here is how you would voice the C Maj13 chord.

This chord adds color to the Major 9 chord to give it a more pleasing sound. You usually see it on a chart when an instrument ensemble includes its added notes. We've left out the 5th interval in this voicing. You can put it back in if you wish.

6

A 6 chord is a major or minor chord with the 6th interval added.

Here's how to play 6 chords.

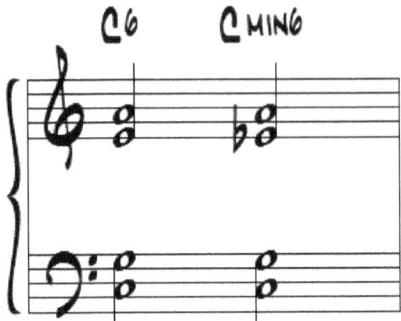

The 6 chord is formed by adding the 6th interval to a major or minor triad and, like the maj7 chord, is a colorful substitution for a major chord. Try it while you're playing.

6/9

The 6/9 chord adds a 6th and a 9th above the root and explicitly excludes the dominant 7 and 5th intervals.

Here's how to play the C6/9 chord.

*teach yourself...*Jazz Piano Comping

In some chord books the 6/9 chord includes the 5th interval. In others it does not. I've never encountered a situation where adding or removing the 5th has any effect on the correctness of the sound. That doesn't mean there's no reason for leaving the 5th out. It's just that I've never run into it.

The main thing to remember is that a 6/9 chord does not include the dominant 7 note, which in a C chord would be B♭.

You learn with experience when you can make these substitutions.

Exercise: Still More Chord Practicing

Once again you'll add to the chord deck you started in Chapter 4 by adding the Maj7, Maj9, Maj13, 6 and 6/9 chords you just learned. These are the cards you want. For each root: C, D♭, D, E♭, F, F♯, G, A♭, A, B♭, and B, write the name of one kind of chord on its own card. That's 60 more cards to add to the deck.

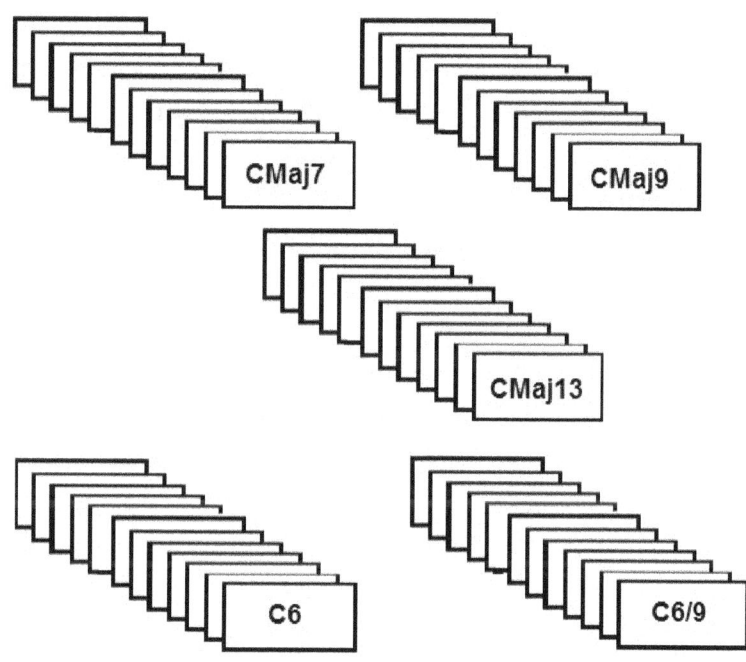

You learned the voicings of these chords for C in this chapter. You have not, however, learned how to voice the chords with roots other than C. So open Appendix A where you can find those voicings.

1. Shuffle these 60 cards into the chord deck. At this point it might be easier to just spread them around on the table and re-stack them.

2. Repeat the practice regimen you learned in Chapter 4 except now use the cards from this and Chapters 4 and 5.

Repeat this exercise until you can play any of these 60 chords by name without thinking about it.

Your chord vocabulary is growing by leaps and bounds, but we're not done.

Chapter 7. Diminished Chords

A diminished chord contains three or four notes with each note being the minor 3rd of the note that precedes it. To make a diminished chord—actually, a dim7 chord; more about that soon—start with a dominant 7 chord such as you learned in Chapter 4 and flat all the notes one-half tone except the root.

There are two kinds of diminished chords. The quality symbol for one is named *dim* and the other is named *dim7*. The diminished chord has three notes. The diminished 7 chord has four notes. We'll discuss only the diminished 7 chord because wherever you see a chord symbol with the suffix *dim*, the diminished 7 chord will fit. Theory scholars might argue with that statement, but in decades of big band and combo playing, I've never found it to be otherwise.

There are only three diminished 7 chords. That's right, only three. There are twelve notes, and each note can be the root of a diminished chord. We'll start with the C family.

Cdim7, E♭dim7, G♭dim7, Adim7

A diminished 7 chord is a root and three notes, each note three half tones above the previous one.

C diminished 7 contains these notes:

C, E♭, G♭, and A

Now, consider the E♭dim7 chord.

Its notes are: E♭, G♭, A, and C

Right away you notice that E♭dim7 contains the same notes as Cdim7 only in the first inversion.

Now look at G♭dim7 and Adim7.

These chords contain these notes: G♭, A, C, E♭, again the same as Cdim7 but in the second and third inversions.

Here are how you would play all four diminished 7 chords from the C, E♭, G♭, A family:

Look at the root notes at the bottoms of the chords. The chords are all the same notes but in different orders. And they are all interchangeable. Wherever one of them is called for on a chart, you can play any of the others. Each one is an inversion (Chapter 3) of the other three.

Don't forget that G♭ and E♭ are also F♯ and D♯ respectively.

Fdim7, A♭dim7, Bdim7, Ddim7

Now, on to the next set of dim7 chords/ Here is Fdim7

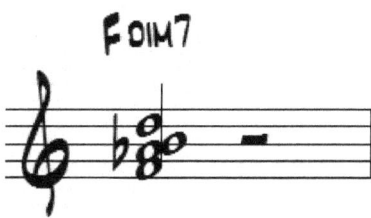

Fdim7 contains these notes: F, A♭, B, D, which are the same notes as in A♭dim7, Bdim7, and Ddim7, which can all be played with the same voicing.

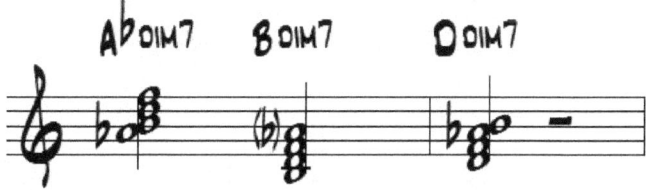

Don't forget that A♭ is also G♯.

Here is how you'd play the diminished 7 chords in the F, A♭, B, D family.

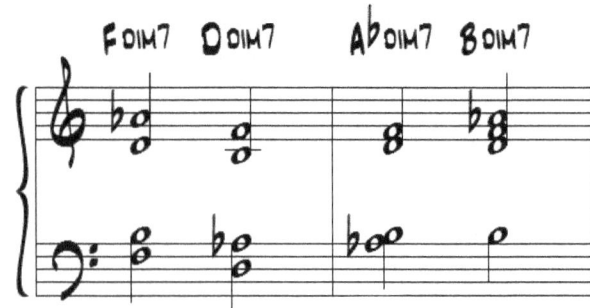

The inversions are not the same as we used in the Cdim family above. This illustrates that you have many choices when you voice chords and the ones being taught here are among them.

Gdim7, B♭dim7, D♭dim7, Edim7

Here is Gdim7.

Gdim7 contains these notes: G, B♭, D♭, E, which are the same notes as in B♭dim7, D♭dim7, and Edim7, which can all be played with the same voicing.

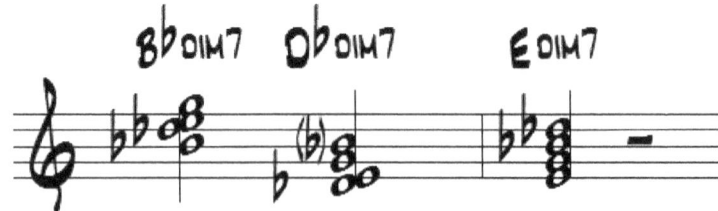

Don't forget that B♭ and D♭ are also A♯ and C♯ respectively.

Here's how to play the diminished 7 chords in the B♭, D♭, E, G family

Diminished 7 chords, when called for on a chart, should be played without colors or substitutions. If you embellish these chords in an arranged ensemble, chances are you'll clash with what the other instruments are playing.

Dim7 Substitutions

Diminished 7 chords are often substituted for chords with flatted 9ths (Chapter 9) and even dominant 7 chords in order to add a modern color to the chord. And those chords are sometimes substituted for dim7 chords.

These common substitutions, for example, are close harmonically and if you play them, few people will notice.

But you can't always do that. There are places where only the diminished 7 chord as written (or one of its inversions) will work. You should not substitute something else. An example is in the last eight measures of Gershwin's *S'Wonderful*.

In the 1980s, I was in Blues Alley, a club in Washington DC, listening to jazz vocalist, Anita O'Day, singing S'Wonderful *in the key of G. When she hit the lyric, "s'marvelous..." at the end, which calls for a Gdim7 chord, the pianist played instead an A7 chord, which has some of the same notes but without that distinctive diminished sound. After a couple choruses like that, Ms. O'Day, clearly irritated at the pianist's inept, in her opinion, interpretation of the song, sang these lyrics for those four measures: "S'Wonderful, G-dim-in-ished sev-en..." arpeggiating the chord downward as she sang its name.*

He didn't get it right on the out chorus either.

Half Diminished (min7 ♭ 5)

The half-diminished chord provides a nice change when used to resolve to a dominant 7 or augmented 7 chord (Chapter 8). It is essentially a min7 chord with its 5th interval flatted. The flatted 5th note makes a nice resolution downward a half tone to the root of the chord being resolved to.

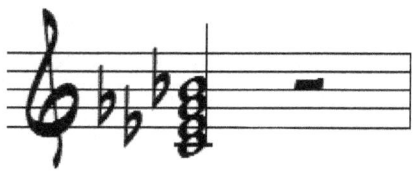

Here is how you would play the Cmin7(♭5) chord):

A close look reveals that min6 chords are first inversions of the min7(♭5) chords. For example, E♭min6 is a first inversion of Cmin7(♭5) as shown here:

Old sheet music for popular songs often substituted the chord symbols of min6 chords for their associated min7(♭5) chords.

When reading those old sheet music tunes from my mother's piano bench, I'd see Fmin6 resolving to G7, for example, but the simple two-clef piano arrangement would show a D as the lowest bass clef note for the first chord.

When I learned more about theory, I opined that they used the old substitutions because publishers understood that typical amateur guitar and ukulele players would be more likely to recognize and play minor 6 chords.

*teach yourself...*Jazz Piano Comping

Exercise: Even More Chord Practicing

Once again you'll add to the chord deck you've been building since Chapter 4 by adding the dim7 and min7(♭5) chords you just learned. These are the cards you want. For each root: C, D♭, D, E♭, F, F♯, G, A♭, A, B♭, and B, write the name of one chord on its own card, this time the dim7 and min7(♭5) chords. That's 24 more cards to add to the deck.

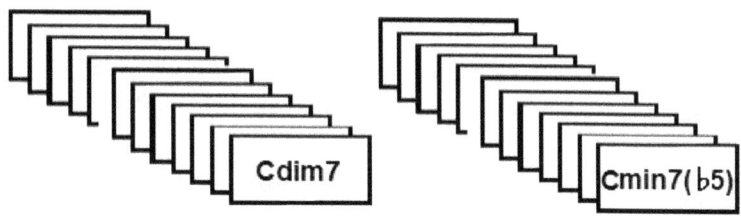

You learned the voicings of these chords in this chapter. You have not, however, learned how to voice the min7(♭5) chords with roots other than C. So open Appendix A where you can find those voicings.

1. Shuffle these 24 cards into the chord deck.
2. Repeat the practice regimen you learned in Chapter 4 except now use the cards from this and the other chapters.

Repeat this exercise until you can play any of these chords by name without thinking about it.

Practice:

Here is *Bill Bailey* (Chapter 4) reharmonized to use some of the chords you learned in this and the previous two chapters:

There's a lot about this chart that is new when you compare it to the same tune in Chapter 4. We still use the half and whole note convention to depict the chord voicings. But we've used the colorful voicings for the chords themselves. And we've added passing chords to give the tune more harmonic variety.

Of course, if you're reading from a band chart, you should play the chords the chart provides to avoid clashes with whatever notes the band is playing. But if it's a lead sheet and a small rhythm section, you have a bit more latitude.

Chapter 8. Augmented and Suspended Chords

The augmented and suspended chords are typically played when the melody note is other than one that fits harmonically into the chord being played.

Augmented

The augmented chord can be named aug, +, or +5. For example, you might see the C augmented chord symbol spelled Caug. C+, or C+5.

Here are the notes in the Caug chord.

Here's how you would play it.

Its purpose is to provide a major chord when the melody note wants to be one half tone up from the major chord's 5th interval.

For example, in *Poor Butterfly* the Caug in measure 5 reflects a C chord with G♯ as the melody note.

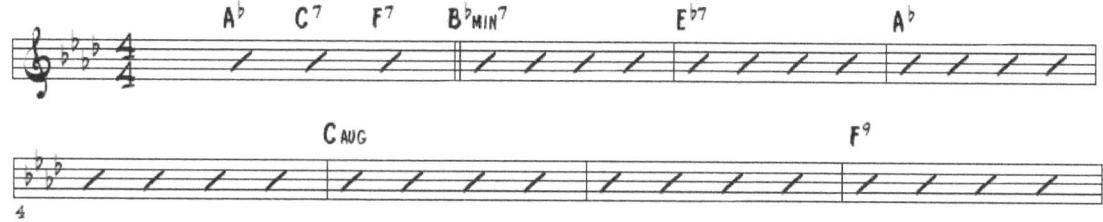

The Caug could also be Caug7 (discussed next) because it resolves to F9.

There are only four augmented chords if you consider the inversions. The three notes in an augmented chord are complementary. Gaug is G, B and E♭. Baug is B, E♭ and G. E♭aug is E♭, G and B.

Augmented 7

This chord is named *augmented 7* which might lead you to believe the 7th is augmented. It isn't, of course. It's a dominant 7 chord with the 5th augmented just as in an augmented chord.

Here are the notes in the Caug7 chord:

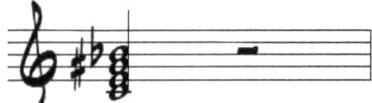

Here's how you would play it.

The augmented 7 chord supports resolving to the next chord in the cycle with the tonic's blue minor 3rd in the melody. It is also used in minor keys in place of the usual dominant 7 to resolve to the minor tonic chord. The augmented 5th of the aug7 chord is also the minor 3rd of the tonic chord.

teach yourself...Jazz Piano Comping

Practice:

You saw a fragment of the 1916 tune *Poor Butterfly*, which has become a jazz standard. The following chart expands on those changes and provides the tune's complete chorus for you to practice.

This tune uses augmented 7 chords in measures 5, 12, and 21.

Note that this chart employs mostly the vanilla chords from Chapter 4 with the occasional Maj7 (Chapter 6) tossed in.

You can refer to the chapters about colorful chords to find substitutions for the vanilla chords to make the accompaniment a bit more interesting not only to you as the player but to listeners as well.

Suspended

A suspended chord is typically a dominant 7 chord with the 3rd left out and the root of the next expected chord substituted for the 3rd. That note is one half-tone above the 3rd.

Here are the notes for Csus.

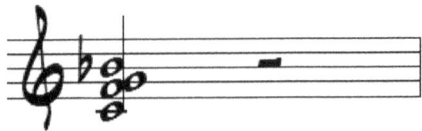

Observe in the Csus chord that an F is where you'd normally expect an E. That F is what provides the suspended sound of the chord.

Here's how you would play the Csus chord.

Note that the sus chord symbol can be spelled Csus4 or C7sus. Another inconsistency in the spelling of chord symbols.

You would use a suspended chord, for example, when the melody note is the root of the tonic chord of the current tonal center (Chapter 12) while the chord is the 5th interval dominant 7.

Exercise: Even More Chord Practicing

Once again you'll add to the chord deck you started in Chapter 4 by adding the aug, aug7 and sus chords you just learned. These are the cards you want. For each root: C, D♭, D, E♭, F, F♯, G, A♭, A, B♭, and B, write the name of one chord on its own card, this time the aug, aug7 and sus chords. That's 36 more cards to add to the deck.

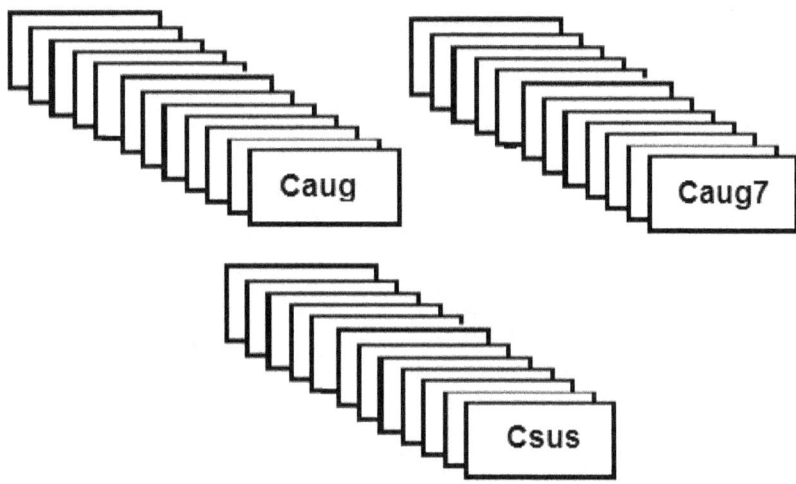

You learned the voicings of these chords in this chapter. You have not, however, learned how to voice the chords with roots other than C. So open Appendix A where you can find those voicings.

1. Shuffle these 36 cards into the chord deck.
2. Repeat the practice regimen you learned in Chapter 4 except now use the cards from this and the other chapters.

Repeat this exercise until you can play any of these chords by name without thinking about it.

teach yourself...Jazz Piano Comping

Practice:

I'm Always Chasing Rainbows was written in 1917 as an adaptation of the slower portion of Chopin's *Fantaisie Impromptu*. It became a hit and was recorded by many artists. Judy Garland sang it in a movie in the early 1940s, capitalizing on her hit, *Somewhere Over the Rainbow* from *The Wizard of Oz*.

You'll see several sus4 chords in this tune, reflecting the use of a 4th melody note against a dominant 7 chord.

Chapter 9. Altered Interval Chords

An *altered interval* chord has one or more of its intervals sharped or flatted. The alterations typically, but not always, represent a sharp or flat deviation from the current tonic's scale in the tune's melody. Sometimes you see them named on a chart when the ensemble's harmonies include them. They are found on piano solo arrangements for the same reason.

From this point on, the example notated chords present only the two-clef voicing for the chords and, as before, they are given for the root C.

Dominant 7 Flat Nine (♭9)

A flat nine chord is a dominant 7 chord with a flatted 9th note added at the top. It provides a modern color to the chord and is often needed when the melody calls for that note.

The flatted 9th note needs to be at the top of the chord to maintain distance from the root note. A flatted 9th is the same note that is one-half step above the root, and putting them too close together makes for dissonance.

Dominant 7 Sharp Nine (♯9)

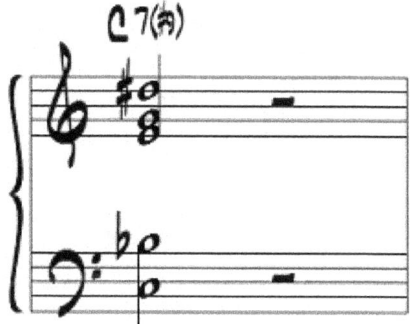

Sharp 9 adds a bluesy feeling to a dominant 7 chord. It adds the tonic's primary blues note, the minor 3rd, to its major chord. Chapter 22 discusses blue notes.

For the sharp 9 to work, the 3rd must be included in the chord. Otherwise, the sharp 9, which is also a flatted 3rd, gives the chord a minor sound. The sharp 9 is best played with that note at the highest position in the form. It needs distance from the major 3rd to avoid dissonance.

Dominant 7 Flat 5 (♭5)

The flatted 5th is believed to be the Holy Grail for be-bop jazz and beyond. But you'll find it in classical music going back centuries. In jazz, a flatted 5th chord is usually called for when the melody note is the flatted 5th of the chord.

You wouldn't play this chord when the tune's melody note is an unflatted 5th interval. But then, it wouldn't be called for on the chart if that were the case. I'm thinking more of when you improvise accompaniments of singers and instrumental soloists.

Exercises

Exercise: Even More Chord Practicing

Once again you'll add to the chord deck you started in Chapter 4 by adding the altered interval chords you just learned. For each root: C, D♭, D, E♭, F, F♯, G, A♭, A, B♭, and B, write the name of one altered interval chord on its own card. That's 36 more cards to add to the deck.

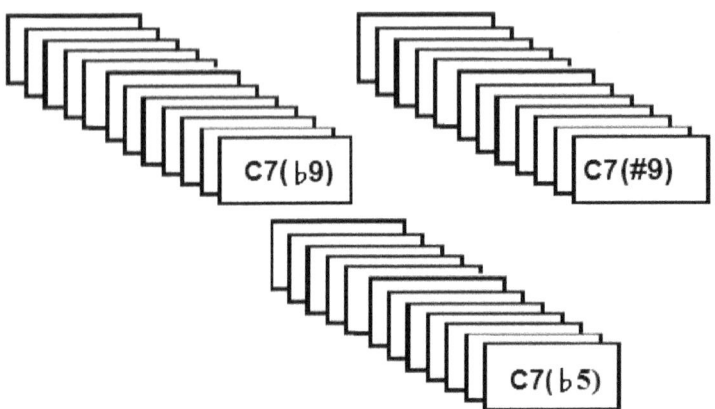

You learned the voicings of the altered interval chords in this chapter. You have not, however, learned how to voice the chords with roots other than C. So open Appendix A where you can find those voicings.

1. Shuffle these cards into the chord deck. It's getting to be a handful, but these are the last cards you'll add.
2. Repeat the practice regimen you learned in Chapter 4 except now use the cards from this and the other chapters.

Repeat this exercise until you can play any of these chords by name without thinking about it.

At this point, if you've carefully and diligently worked all the exercises in these chapters about chords and practiced all the tunes, you know all the piano chords you'll probably ever need, assuming you have broadened what you learned to all twelve root notes. There are others but I doubt you'll need them. If you run across one on a chart, Google its name to see if the Internet can explain it.

Chapter 10. Rootless Chords

I won't spend a lot of time on these, because they're simple, assuming you've worked your way through the previous chapters in Part II. I'll give a couple examples, but you won't be adding cards to your chord deck and you won't have to refer to Appendix A. You already know all the chords you need. To play a rootless chord, do this: Assume the chord position and raise your left pinkie.

That's right, lift the finger that you usually use to play the root note—if it's other than your pinkie, lift the finger on the root—in any of the voicings you've learned up to now and play the chord. Here are some examples.

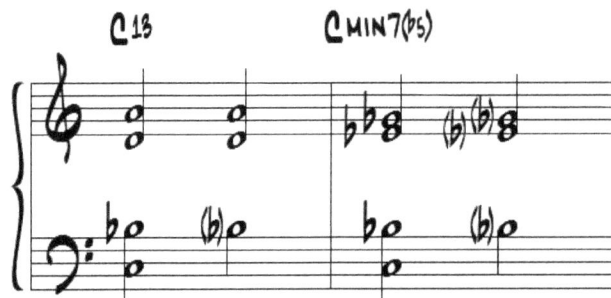

The first measure in the example above shows a C13 chord in root position and as a rootless chord. The second measure shows the same thing with the Cmin7(♭5) chord.

Why rootless chords? There are two occasions I can cite.

First, you are in a rhythm section with a strong bass player who dependably lays down the bass line. Your constant use of a root note in your chords can interfere with what the bass player is playing. You might even hear from that player. "Get the heck out of the root position." It's happened to me.

The second use of rootless chords is when you are playing in the style of more modern players such as the modal styles of Bill Evans, Chick Corea and others. They used rootless chords even when there was no bass player or even when the bass player avoided root notes too.

If you aspire to that kind of playing, by all means run all the exercises in the previous chapters in Part II to learn the chords' rootless voicings. As I said, it's easy. Just lift your pinkie.

Practice:

Here's the old 1917 tune, *Back Home Again in Indiana* by James F. Hanley, the changes of which have been used in several jazz tunes.

Play these changes first without backing track accompaniment (a recorded rhythm section playing the tune as Appendix B explains) to see how well they define the underlying harmonies of the tune without any root notes.

Play these changes along with the backing track software playing the same tune. Let the bass in the backing track lay down the bottom. In this arrangement, we have many colorful chords and none of them have root notes. We use colorful voicings to add substance when there is no root.

PART III Music Theory

Part III is about the dreaded subject, m*usic theory*. You learned about scales and chords in Part II. Those are to theory as nouns and verbs are to prose.

Theory is about why chords fit where they fit and sound right when they sound right. It's also about what to play next based on what you just played or heard. That's what an understanding of theory provides.

You know what to play next.

And one cardinal rule overrides all others:

If it sounds right, it's right

If you already know formal music theory at an advanced level, you might want to skip to Part IV. But I urge you to scan Part III just so you'll know we're on the same page.

You can play tunes without knowing what Part III teaches. You can read chord symbols from charts the way Part II teaches and plug happily away. That's well and good if you play only from charts. But if you want to jam when someone names a tune you've heard but have no chart for, you need a touch of theory so you'll know which chord is expected next based on the melodic and harmonic contexts in which you *hear* the chord.

You need to be able to play "by ear."

Part III explains the two elements at the core of music theory without all the formal jargon. These elements are *harmonic context* and *tonal centers*. There is overlap in these subjects. Keep in mind, however, that musicians don't usually hang around the bandstand or studio talking about such matters in these terms. They just talk about the "changes," which Part IV discusses. But harmonic contexts and tonal centers are the framework in which the changes exist and are the foundation of music theory.

Chapter 11. Harmonic Contexts

Part II taught you about the major, minor, dominant 7 and minor 7 chords and their variations. Now we'll put those chords into a *harmonic context*. We have to use them and others like them to play tunes within the proper harmonic contexts. To do that we must address how the chords *resolve* to one another.

An old folk tale helps to explain chord resolution.

In the story, Mozart, according to some versions, and Chopin, according to others, lies in bed trying to get some rest. Some versions put the composer on his deathbed to dramatize and thus emphasize the point of the story.

The story goes as follows:

> *While Mozart/Chopin is trying to fall asleep, someone downstairs is at the piano playing a tune. The pianist takes the piece up to the next to the last chord and then, for one reason or another, gets up from the piano without completing it and walks away.*
>
> *The composer, unable to sleep while the incomplete tune remains unresolved, leaves his bed, rushes to the piano, and plays the last chord, after which he returns to bed and goes to sleep.*

Why would he do that? To *resolve* the incomplete harmonic sequence that's been left unspoken, or hanging. To *hear* the ending. To finish it.

The foundation of harmonic context can be found in the resolution of one chord to the next and in the patterns of chord changes or sequences that form passages (Chapter 16) in tunes.

Chord Resolution

Here's what *chord resolution* is. The listener hears a melody or some changes and expects to hear them resolve with a very specific sound, with the note or chord that completes the passage.

Of course, it's difficult to explain in words what something sounds like. But we can use examples that you can play on your piano.

We'll play chord changes that you'd expect to resolve to a tonic, but that go somewhere else, perhaps to another set of changes. But eventually there should be a closing resolution, and you hear what you expect to hear.

There is a way to understand resolution, a way that I can describe it by using something with which everyone is familiar.

teach yourself...Jazz Piano Comping

Exercise:

Sing or play on the piano the last line of *Take Me Out to the Ballgame* as shown above, but don't sing or play the final note. Leave that note hanging. Ask anyone within earshot to sing what they expect to hear. They'll sing "game," and unless they are tone deaf, it will be a C.

Now we'll add the changes, which fit with the end of *Take Me Out to the Ballgame* in C.

Exercise:

Are there chords up there you haven't learned? No, there aren't. You have indeed learned them, it's just that you learned them in a C root. Here's how you can voice them all.

Sing the phrase, this time playing the chords on the piano to accompany yourself on the piano. Sing it all the way to the end.

That last chord, the C, is your resolved chord. The G7 makes you expect to hear the C chord played. Leave it out, and Chopin and Mozart will fall over each other, running downstairs.

Another lesson here: This notation uses two different voicings for the C chord. They both have their root on C in the bass clef, and the E on the bottom line of the treble clef, but the G is positioned differently for each incidence of the C chord. The only good reason to do that other than to show it being done is because the lead lines in the last four measures descend, and the accompaniment sounds better this way.

From this point forward, whenever you see a chord in this book that you cannot voice on your own, refer to Appendix A to find its voicing.

The resolving chord symbol in a passage is usually named with the note that ends the passage. So, in the key of C, the last note of the tune's melody is usually C because that's what the listener expects to hear, and the last chord is probably C major. Likewise, if the tune is in C minor, the last melody note would be C and the last chord would be C minor.

There are many exceptions to this rule, all of which could confuse you at this point, so we won't delve into them. Let's keep it simple for now.

The Cycle/Circle of 4ths/5ths

What makes one chord suggest the next chord in sequence? What elements in a chord generate the tension that wants to be resolved by the next one? And which second chord does the first chord suggest?

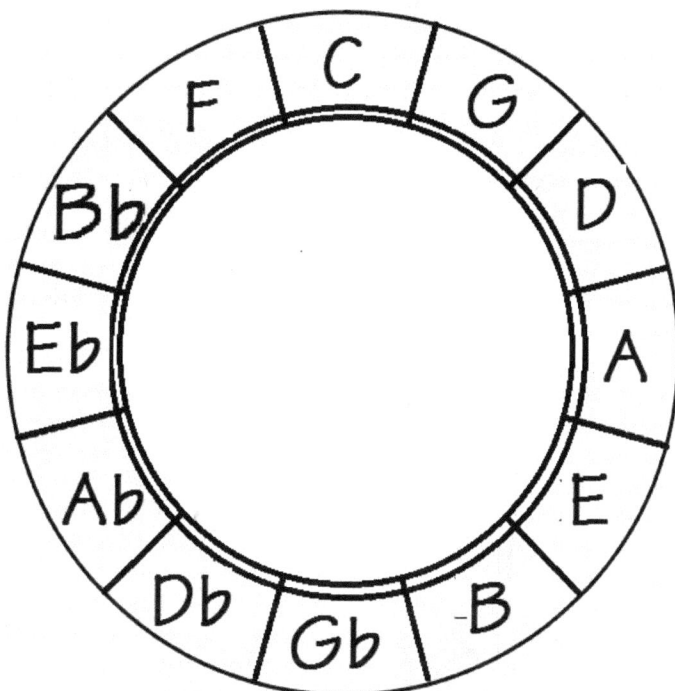

You've probably seen variations on this illustration in other works about musical theory. Harmonic resolution involves *tension* in the tune's harmonic context which must be resolved, usually by a chord from the counter-clockwise adjacent note in the circle.

Clockwise, the wheel depicts a cycle of 5ths. Counter-clockwise, it depicts a cycle of 4ths, which is what you will be most concerned with.

If you could rotate the circle clockwise, you'd see the next chord in the cycle at the top. C resolves to F, which resolves to B♭ and so on.

But the circle is just a picture. It doesn't make sense until you hear it. And without multi-media, you can't hear a picture. One picture might be worth a thousand words in prose, but in music, two notes are worth a thousand pictures.

As you navigate the circle in a clockwise direction, each note, when looked at as the tonic note of its own major scale and the root note of its own chord, leads to the dominant note—the 5th—in that scale. Navigating counter-clockwise, each successive note is the subdominant note—the 4th—in the previous note's scale.

Resolving Chords

The exercises above showed you how the G7 chord in *Take Me Out to the Ballgame* resolves to the C chord. What does it mean when we say, for example, that G *resolves* to C? Those single notes don't fully explain the concept of resolution. Each one is a tonic note to a chord, and the chords' other notes—thirds, 5ths, and dominant 7ths—are what create the tensions that need to be resolved by the playing of a consequent chord and are what lured Chopin or Mozart from his deathbed to finish the resolution that someone else left unresolved.

The most important intervals in a dominant 7 chord are the 3rd and 7th.

Omit either of them and you remove the harmonic relevance of the chord to the rest of the passage that hosts the chord. Those notes are even more important than a chord's root and its 5th. A listener's brain will infer those tones if you leave them out. But leave out the 3rd, and the listener can't distinguish between a dominant 7 and a minor 7. Leave out the 7th and there is nothing from which to resolve to the next chord.

Exercise:

Play this C chord followed by this F chord and leave some silent space between. Maybe a couple seconds.

Not much about the C to F sequence creates any tension. You could quit after the C chord and nobody would care. Mozart and Chopin would stay in their beds. Nothing connects the two chords. The C could end a passage and the F could begin the next passage. At C, the ear says, "This is done. Move on." At F, the ear says, "We're at the start of another harmonic journey. Proceed."

It isn't always that way—little in music theory is always the same way—but as a general rule, it applies.

teach yourself...Jazz Piano Comping

Exercise:

Play the same two chords but add the dominant 7th note B♭ to the C chord.

During the pause between chords, did you hear the tension? You can't walk away from that. It begs to be resolved. When you finally do play the F chord, the tension is resolved and the changes are complete. Nobody needs to come storming out of the bedroom to hit that missing F chord.

The effect just demonstrated is harmonic resolution in a nutshell. The chords in a set of changes fit together because of one thing: they sound right within the context of the tune, which means they sound like what the listener expects to hear.

The resolution that the tension demands is found in the note you added to the C chord. That B♭ dominant 7th demands to be resolved one half tone down to the F chord's A, its 3rd interval.

Consequently, the resolution of C7 to F is not C to F as the cycle of 4th's wheel would indicate as much as it is B♭ to A. If you leave those notes out of the changes, nothing has been resolved because no tension has been generated. Try it.

Exercise:

Play these two chords in succession as you did above.

Hear the difference? With no dominant 7 (B♭) in the C chord, no tension is created. With no 3rd (A) in the F chord, there is nothing to resolve to.

If you put the dominant 7 (B♭) back into the C chord, the tension returns. Listeners will accept your F chord without its 3rd interval. Their brains will infer the E.

Now don't jump to conclusions. All B♭s in chords in which B♭s occur do not demand to be resolved to chords that have an A. However, dominant 7th notes do wish to resolve to the 3rd of the next chord in the circle/cycle.

Chapter 12. Tonal Centers

A tune's harmonic contexts are each defined by one or more *tonal centers*, sequences of chords that typically resolve to a tonic chord, and a tune can comprise multiple tonal centers.

We know that a tune is usually written and played in a *key*. Those reading music know that the key of the composition or of an arrangement of the tune is expressed in its *key signature*, a number of sharps or flats encoded at the beginning of the standard notation. The key is usually the root of the concluding chord and the last note of the melody. Usually, but not always. Two tunes that end up in a different key than the one they start with are *Unforgettable* and *Why Did I Choose You*. Vocalists love to end a tune on the signature key's 3rd interval. Don't ask me why. They'll hit the 5th, too, and, if it's a blues, (Chapter 14) they might even end on the signature key's dominant 7th. To further confuse you, be-bop horn players like to end on its flatted 5th.

The *original* key is usually defined as the key in which the tune was originally published and is usually chosen so that the tonal range of the melody matches the vocal range of the typical male vocalist. Sorry, ladies, that's just how it's done. For purposes of this discussion, the original key is the one in which we are playing it, the one identified on charts by the key signature (Chapter 18), or the one called out by whoever in the band calls the tunes and the keys.

Harmonic Contexts

Chapter 11 discussed harmonic contexts. Now let's view them as multiple contexts that define a tune, what we call *tonal centers*.

A tune can be written in more than one key although it usually has only one key signature. It can have phrases that modulate from the original key to a different one, usually returning to and ending with the original key. (There are exceptions. Don't worry about them now.) These modulations change the tune's tonal center.

A tonal center, also called a *key center*, is the key in which a passage of a tune is played when it has modulated from the original key. Such modulations do not change the key signature. They just happen, and you play along with them, fully expecting the tune to find its way back to the original key, the original tonal center.

An example is the bridge of the old tune, *Blue Moon* in the key of E♭ and shown here in a chord chart (Chapter 18).

Blue Moon is one of two tunes that kids learn to play in duo on the piano. The other one is Heart and Soul. One kid plays the bass: note, chord, note, chord in the key of C. The other kid plays the melody. My cousin and I almost drove my aunt to drink with those renditions when we were kids.

If you're unfamiliar with (too young for) *Blue Moon*, look it up on YouTube where you'll find several versions. It was written in the 1930s by Richard Rogers and has had many renditions. Originally, it was a ballad. Subsequently it made the charts with an up-tempo do-wop version and has been covered by Elvis, Sinatra, and every lounge singer since then.

Years back a local piano player was taking flying lessons. He almost had his license and he told the band's trumpet player that he'd like to take him for a ride after he got certified. The trumpet player pulled back and said, "You're nuts if you think I'm going up in an airplane with a piano player who doesn't know the changes to the bridge to Blue Moon.*"*

The bridge, which runs from measure 17 through measure 24, stays in tonal center E♭ for the first four measures but with a common set of chord changes, in this case, Fmin7, B♭7, E♭, Cmin7, the 2, 5, 1, 6 changes. The bridge then modulates to tonal center G♭ before returning to tonal center E♭.

That's two measures during which the tune is not in its original key. As complex as it might seem at first glance, this is a simple example, and you might wonder what the fuss is about. It illustrates harmonic behavior common to jazz and standard tunes. Some tunes stray much further from the original and move into multiple tonal centers before finding their way back to the original. The point is, you need to be aware of these changes, be able to recognize not only that the tonal center is changing, but what key it is in, and be able to play in that key.

The bridge to *Have you Met Miss Jones* changes tonal centers six times in eight measures, including the change from the signature key of F to B♭ in the first measure of the bridge, making it back to the original at the end of the bridge. Find a rendition of the tune on YouTube to hear what happens in the bridge, and follow along with this extract of the bridge. We are in the key of F in this example but the bridge begins in the B♭ tonal center.

The illustration shows the tonal centers above the measures for each melodic phrase. When the bridge begins in the first measure shown in the illustration, its first measure goes into the B♭ tonal center. The second measure of the bridge modulates into a G♭ tonal center which it stays in for one more measure. The fourth measure goes into D, the sixth measure into G♭ again, and the eighth measure returns the refrain to the original key of F.

There are many tunes in the jazz and standards repertoire that wander all over the tonal center map. Among them are *Joy Spring, All the Things You Are, Cherokee,* and *You Go to my Head*.

How do you identify a tonal center? Usually (but not always) the phrase in question resolves to the tonal center's major chord as happens with each of the tonal center changes shown for *Miss Jones*'s bridge. Remember from above, a tonal center is the key in which a passage of a tune is played when it has modulated from the original key

Why do you care? Can't you just play the chords as written and not worry about an abstract theoretical detail such as the tonal center? Yes, you can if all you are doing is playing along while a singer or instrumentalist carries the tune. But if you ever move into taking solos—and virtually every jazz piano player does—the scales and tonal centers will suggest to you which improvised notes fit with each phrase of the tune.

PART IV The Changes

Part III taught you why chords resolve from one chord to the next. You learned about harmonic contexts and tonal centers. Part IV presents the actual chord changes, some typical sequences and progressions of chords you play that comprise a tune.

Composers draw from their own vocabulary of harmonic sequences when they write tunes. Players come to recognize the patterns, and how and when they apply. Most of your playing will employ passages of changes that you've already played in other tunes.

Chapter 13. Common Progressions

Tunes are written with patterns of chord changes, and there are many such patterns that are common and well-known to musicians. This chapter discusses the three most often seen progressions in contemporary music, including standards, country and western, jazz, and popular hits.

You learn a new notation convention here for the naming of chords. This notation uses Roman numerals to identify a chord's root. The numeral is an interval relative to the tonal center's root and if the numeral is upper case, the chord is major; if the numeral is lower case, the chord is minor. With the exception of the root of I (one), the chords are assumed to be dominant 7 or minor 7 chords.

In this notation, **I** represents the tonic of the tonal center, **ii** is the minor 7 chord with a root of the 2nd interval of the tonal center, and **V** is the dominant 7 chord with a root of the 5th interval of the tonal center.

For example, in the tonal center of C, ii-V-I would be Dmin7, G7, C.

These identifiers are verbal shortcuts for the changes. You don't see them printed anywhere. They exist so musicians can communicate about chord changes. The notation style is similar to the so-called "Nashville Notation" style that country-western stringed instrument players use to notate tunes.

Two-Five

"ii-V" also called two-five when spoken, is not always addressed in discussions of chord changes. Many people go straight into "ii-V-I," which is where we're headed. But ii-V is an interesting topic. It goes like this:

Wherever a dominant 7 chord is called for, if there is enough space in the rhythm, insert the chord's subdominant minor 7 before the dominant 7 chord.

Like when you see this:

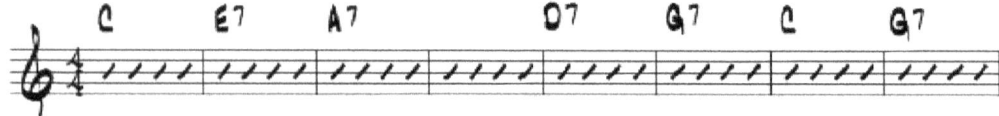

Those are the vanilla changes to the first 8 measures of the old standard, *Five Foot Two, Eyes of Blue*.

I won't provide a complete chart because although the tune was originally published in 1914, a more popular version came out in 1925. I don't want to go to the wall with anybody's lawyers.

Take each dominant 7 chord and insert its subdominant minor 7 chord ahead of it. If needed, review the Cycle/Circle of 5ths/4ths in Chapter 11. Remember our discussion with scales? The 4th interval in a scale is the *subdominant*, and 5th interval is the *dominant*. This is what you get:

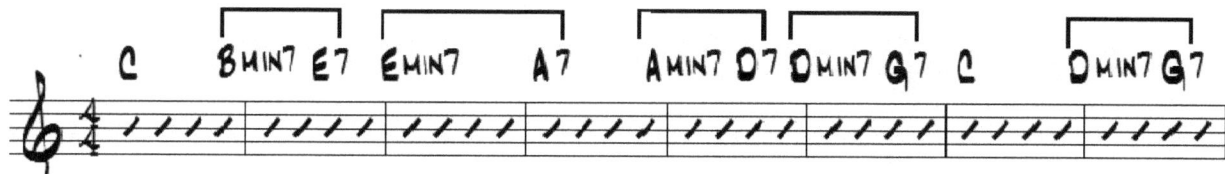

The brackets show where each chord was replaced by two chords. The result is a fuller expression of the harmony that rarely clashes with the melody. (If it does, you'll hear it, endure the singer's glare, and never do it again.) You can further color all the chords with 9ths and 13ths as you wish to gain an even lusher harmonic sound.

Exercise:

- Play the vanilla version of *Five Foot Two*
- Play the version that employs ii-V substitutions
- Change each min7 chord to a min9 and each 7 chord to a 13. Play this newer version.

Two-Five-One

"ii-V," discussed above doesn't always resolve to "I," the tonic of the tonal center, but most times it does, which brings us here.

The chord changes named "ii-V-I" and spoken "two-five-one" are the cornerstone of jazz harmonic construction as well as other music forms that depend on more than just the tonic-subdominant-dominant three-chord set. You saw it in the examples we've discussed in previous chapters. Complete books have been written about ii-V-I and virtually every book about playing jazz on any instrument includes a discussion that addresses ii-V-I.

Believe it or not, *much of your jazz playing involves playing simple ii-V-I changes*. Learn them and assimilate them into your playing, and you'll be comfortable with the majority of tunes you'll be called upon to accompany.

ii-V-I Basics

To understand ii-V-I, consider again the major scale. We'll use the key of C as usual.

C, D, E, F, G, A, B

Consequently, ii-V-I refers to the 2nd, 5th, and 1st intervals in the scale. In the key of C, ii-V-I is D, G, C.

In this notation, lowercase Roman numerals designate a minor chord and uppercase designates a major chord. Again in C, ii-V-I becomes Dmin, G, C.

*teach yourself...*Jazz Piano Comping

But wait. There's more. The ii and V shorthand notations represent dominant 7 chords. The I represents a major chord. Nothing in the shorthand tells you that; it's simply understood. So, given that ambiguity, the ii-V-I for the key of C is, finally:

Dmin7, G7, C

The following table illustrates ii-V-I for all twelve major keys.ii-V-I

Major Key	ii-V-I Changes
A	Bmin7, E7, A
B♭	Cmin7, F7, B♭
C	Dmin7, G7, C
D♭	E♭min7, A♭7, D♭
D	Emin7, A7, D
E♭	Fmin7, B♭7, E♭
E	F#min7, B7, E
F	Gmin7, C7, F
G♭	A♭min7, D♭7, G♭
G	Amin7, D7, G
A♭	B♭min7, E♭7, A♭

The following changes are ii-V-I in the key of C.

Exercise:

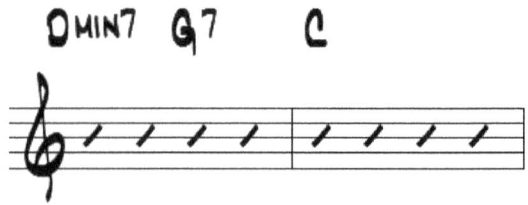

Play these chords repetitively, two beats for the first two chords each and four beats for the third chord.

teach yourself...Jazz Piano Comping

Here is the colorful ii-V-I in C.

Exercise:

Play these changes repetitively as you did the vanilla version.

Practice:

Here are all the ii-V-I changes in ascending chromatic order. Each two-measure pair is in the tonal center of the chord in the second measure.

1. Play the ii-V-I changes presented here in the ascending order chromatically as the

*teach yourself...*Jazz Piano Comping

chart shows

2. Choose and play the two-measure sets in random order

3. Say the names of the chords out loud as you play them. This practice will help you put the chord names and their shapes under your fingers into your so-called *associative memory*, that part of your brain that associates paired definitions such as "dime" and "ten cents" and so on.

Practice:

The ii-V-I changes are presented here in ascending order chromatically. This time you don't see the voicings. You are given only the chord symbols with slash notation. We'll do it mostly this way from this point forward. If you come across a chord you don't know, look it up in Appendix A.

1. Play the ii-V-I changes presented here in the ascending order chromatically as the chart shows

2. Chose and play the two-measure sets in random order

3. Say the names of the chords out loud as you play them.

Repetitive II-V

This is about one of those times when "ii-V" does not resolve to "I." A common idiom in standard tunes is to repeat the ii-V changes multiple times before resolving to I. An example is *Honeysuckle Rose,* usually played in F. Here are the first five measures to illustrate the practice:

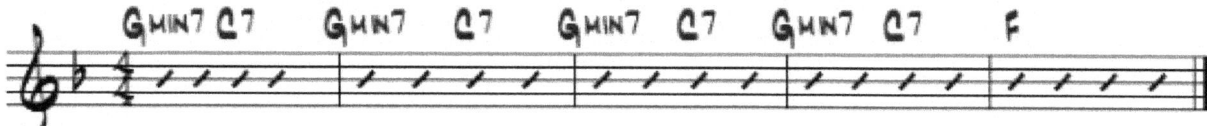

The tonal center for all five measures is F. The tune delays, however, the resolution and extends the tension by repeating the ii-V changes, Gmin7 to C7, three times before letting the third C7 resolve to the F.

Cherokee Bridge

The bridge to *Cherokee* demonstrates another ii-V-I variation. More information on bridges will be presented in Chapter 16. The tonal centers are shown in brackets above the staff.

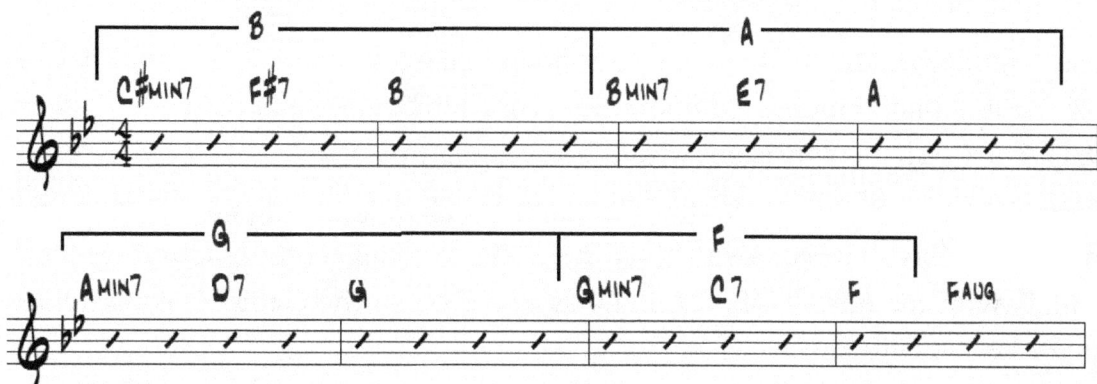

The tune is in B♭, but the bridge launches into the B tonal center without any modulation to resolve to it. It stays there for two measures and modulates into the A tonal center. This is interesting because the ii of tonal center A is Bmin7. The modulation happens when the tonic (B) of the previous tonal center is changed from a major chord to a minor 7 with the same root —B to Bmin7. The bridge repeats that pattern twice more, giving two measures to each tonal center. A to Amin7 and G to Gmin7. The tonal centers modulate down a whole step at a time: B to A to G to F. The Faug chord of the last measure of the bridge then resolves to the original tonal center, B♭.

ii-V-i in Minor Keys

So far we've concentrated on ii-V-I changes as they apply to major key tonal centers. As you might expect, you can use the changes to resolve to a minor tonal center as well, which is spelled ii-V-i and pronounced the same as the major version, "two-five-one." The tune itself doesn't have to be in a minor key to use a ii-V-i, although it can.

First, let's look at a C minor scale.

C minor has three flats, the same flat notes as E♭ major, and the signature key of C minor shares the key signature with E♭. That's why C minor is called the *relative minor* key of E♭ and E♭ is the *relative* major of C. Add that bit of knowledge to your collection of things you don't need to know.

The scale just shown is the C *natural* minor scale. There are two others, the *harmonic* and *melodic* minor scales. More about them soon.

Here are the ii-V-i changes in C minor.

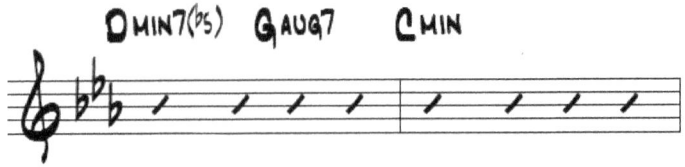

Two things to remember about ii-V-i:

- Usually, but not always, the ii chord in these changes has its 5th interval flatted as shown here. If the tonal center is C minor, the ii chord is Dmin7(♭5) (Chapter 7), with the notes D, F, A♭, C. That is consistent with the key signature.

- Often, but not always, the V chord in the ii-V-i changes is augmented (Chapter 8), which means its 5th is sharped, also shown here. If the tonal center is C minor, the V chord is Gaug7, with the notes G, B, D#, F. D# is also E♭, so the Gaug7 is consistent with the C minor key signature as well.

The third of the V chord keeps its original tone, which it needs to resolve to the i chord. This might seem inconsistent with the key signature, but it is consistent with, for example, the so-called *harmonic* minor key scale, in C minor for this example.

C, D, E♭, F, G, A♭, B, C

The following table illustrates ii-V-i for all twelve minor keys.

Key	ii-V-i changes
A minor	Bmin7(♭5), Eaug7, Amin
B♭ minor	Cmin7(♭5), Faug7, B♭min
C minor	Dmin7(♭5), Gaug7, Cmin
D♭ minor	E♭min7(♭5), A♭aug7, D♭min
D minor	Emin7(♭5), Aaug7, Dmin

teach yourself...Jazz Piano Comping

E♭ minor	Fmin7(♭5), B♭aug7, E♭min
E minor	F#min7(♭5), Baug7, Emin
F minor	Gmin7(♭5), Caug7, Fmin
G♭ minor	A♭min7(♭5), D♭aug7, G♭min
G minor	Amin7(♭5), Daug7, Gmin
A♭ minor	B♭min7(♭5), E♭aug7, A♭min

Here are the ii-V-i changes for each of the minor tonal centers. Once again you get only the chord symbols and slash notation. To voice these chords see Appendix A.

Minor flat five and augmented chords are essential to jazz harmonies. Chapters 7 and 8

ii-V-i Exercises

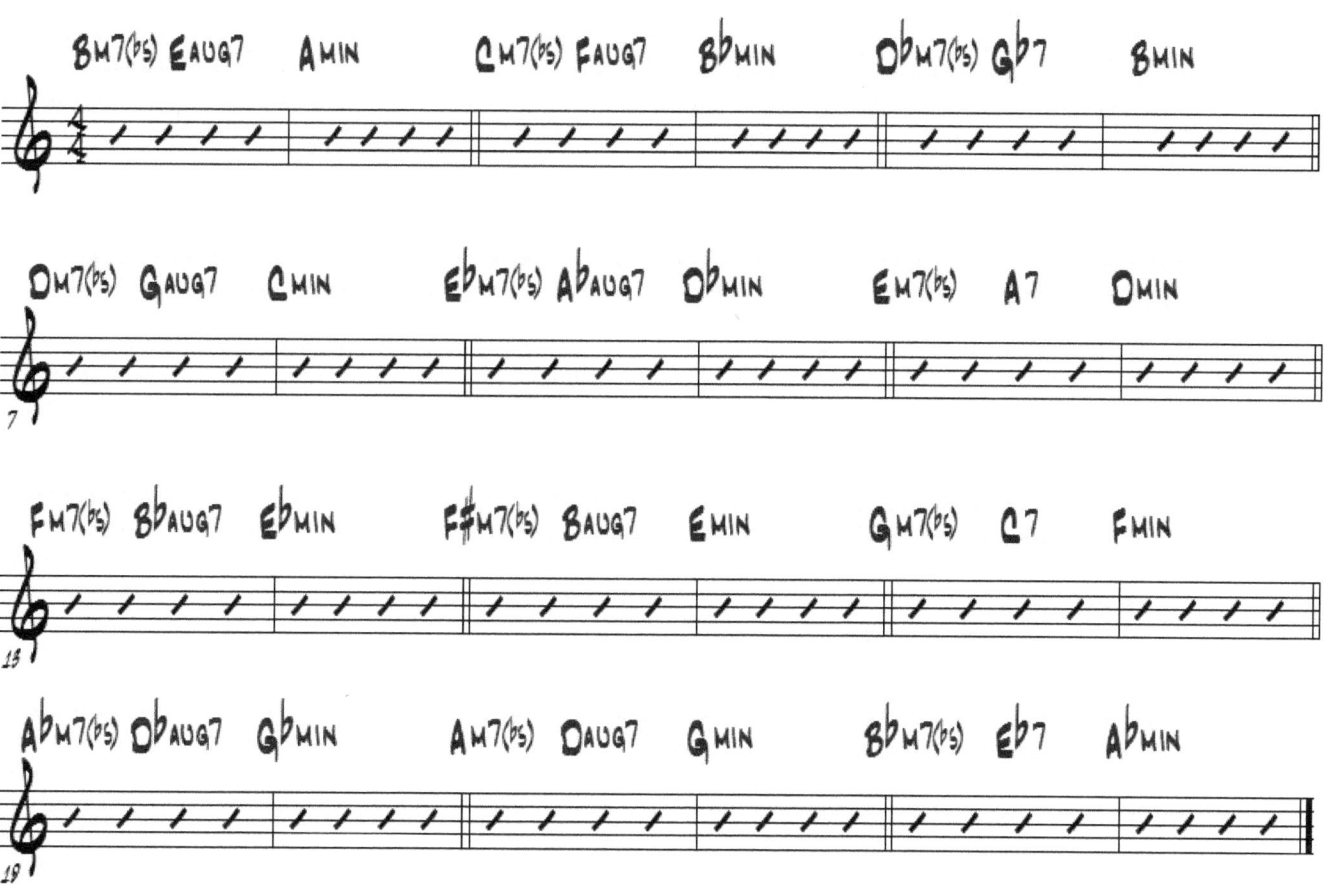

73

As often as not, the V chord is not augmented but only a dominant 7. It depends on the melody, the harmonic context, and the band's interpretation. Keep an eye and ear on the changes that have been written down or agreed to.

One-Six-Two-Five

If ii-V-I are the cornerstone of jazz harmonies, 1-6-2-5 changes, which are the tonic, the 6th interval chord, the 2nd interval chord and the 5th interval chord and usually communicated with Arabic numerals as shown here, are the foundation. Countless old tunes use the 1-6-2-5 changes for their refrains, among them, *Blue Moon, Heart and Soul, The Devil and the Deep Blue Sea, I Got Rhythm* (Chapter 15, and many more.

The only changes more common are the Blues (Chapter 14). The 1-6-2-5 changes are so common in jazz and standards that you will come to recognize them as soon as you see them on a chart.

Here are the changes in the key of F:

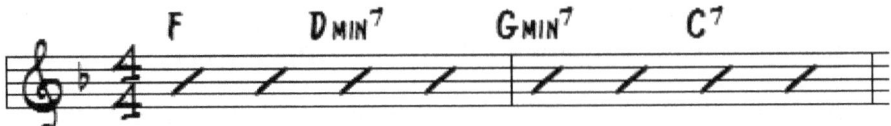

Often, you'll substitute a dominant 7 chord for the minor 7 chord in the first measure. That would make these changes: F, D7, Gmin7, C7.

Exercise:

Practice the 1-6-2-5 changes repetitively. It might seem like you are playing a vamp, which is a repetitive intro (Chapter 16) to or an interlude within a tune awaiting a go-ahead signal from the leader.

There's not much more to 1-6-2-5 than that. You'll use the changes many times in your playing, in the refrains of some tunes, in the bridges (Chapter 16) of others. You'll use them for introductions, turnarounds (Chapter 16), and interludes whenever someone wants to talk to the audience while there's music playing in the background.

The following table illustrates 1-6-2-5 for all twelve major keys.

Key	1-6-2-5 Changes
A	A, F#, Bmin7, E7
B♭	B♭, Gmin7, Cmin7, F7
C	C, Amin7, Dmin7, G7
D♭	D♭, B♭min7, E♭min7, A♭7
D	D, Bmin7, Emin7, A7

E♭	E♭, Cmin7, Fmin7, B♭7
E	E, C#min7, F#min7, B7
F	F, Dmin7, Gmin7, C7
G♭	G♭, E♭min7, A♭min7, D♭7
G	G, Emin7, Amin7, D7
A♭	A♭, Fmin7, B♭min7, E♭7

teach yourself...Jazz Piano Comping

Practice:

The 1917 tune *Indian Summer* by Victor Herbert has become a jazz standard and employs the 1-6-2-5 changes. You'll find more uses of them in the Rhythm Changes (Chapter 15).

Chapter 14. The Blues

The 12-bar *blues* is among the most commonly used chord changes in traditional jazz. It is also a staple of country-western and old time rock 'n' roll. There are several variations to the blues, usually depending on the kind of blues being played.

Blues has its foundations in field and gospel songs from the South, heard toward the end of the nineteenth century. Composer W.C. Handy immortalized blues changes by bringing them into mainstream popular music. His tunes *St. Louis Blues, Memphis Blues,* and others used the basic blues changes and set the standard that's been followed for more than a century.

Major Blues

Here is the traditional twelve-bar major blues chord changes in the key of G. We'll begin with a chord chart (Chapter 18) so you can become accustomed to the format you'll read on gigs.

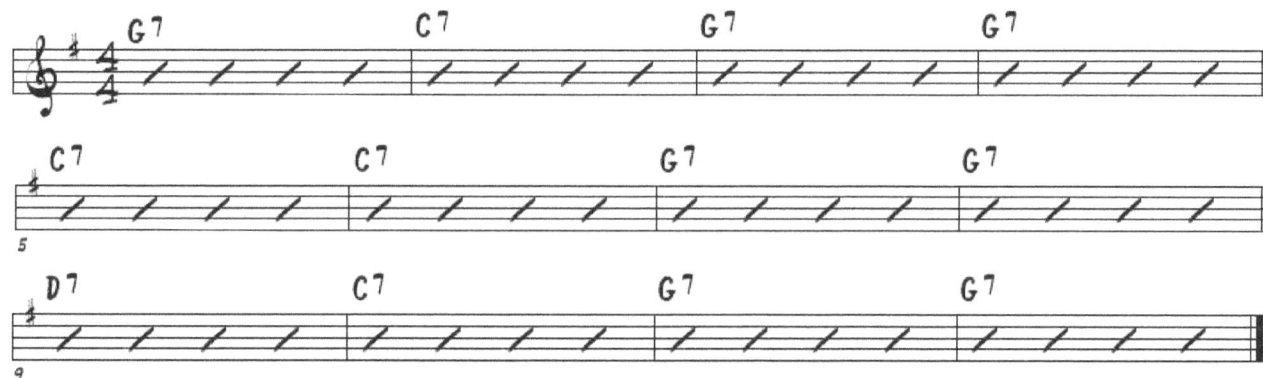

In some 12-bar blues versions, particularly in the old time rock 'n' roll genre, the second measure remains on the tonic chord, which is G7 in this example. The first rock tune I recall hearing, *Rock Around the Clock*, stays with the tonic.

Exercise:

Play *Blues in G* from the chart above until you have the changes memorized. The idea is to impress into your harmonic and muscle memories the associations between the chord symbols and their keyboard voicings.

Exercise:

With the blues under your belt, practice the changes at various tempos from slow, down and dirty (approx. 70 beats per minute) to a top speed swing tempo (approx. 200 bpm). Don't worry if the faster tempo doesn't come to you right away. Get it going as fast as you can and then set it aside for a while.

Recall from Chapter 5 that you can use a 9th wherever you see a 7th and vice versa. The two chords are interchangeable within the harmonic context of the tonal center. Play them side by side to hear the common harmonic sound and the coloring difference that adding the 9 (C) gives to the sound.

Practice:

Now we'll add colors to illustrate the use of altered intervals in the Blues. Here's a version with several altered interval changes. Compare these with the ones you just learned in Chapters 14 and will learn in Chapter 17.

The most frequently played blues are in F, B♭, and G, in that order of precedence, so those are the ones you should be most familiar with. Jazz players love the key of F, calling it the *mother key*.

The 12-bar blues changes have many variations. You'll learn about some of them in Chapter 17.

Minor Blues

You can play the twelve-bar blues in minor keys, too. Here are the changes in G minor.

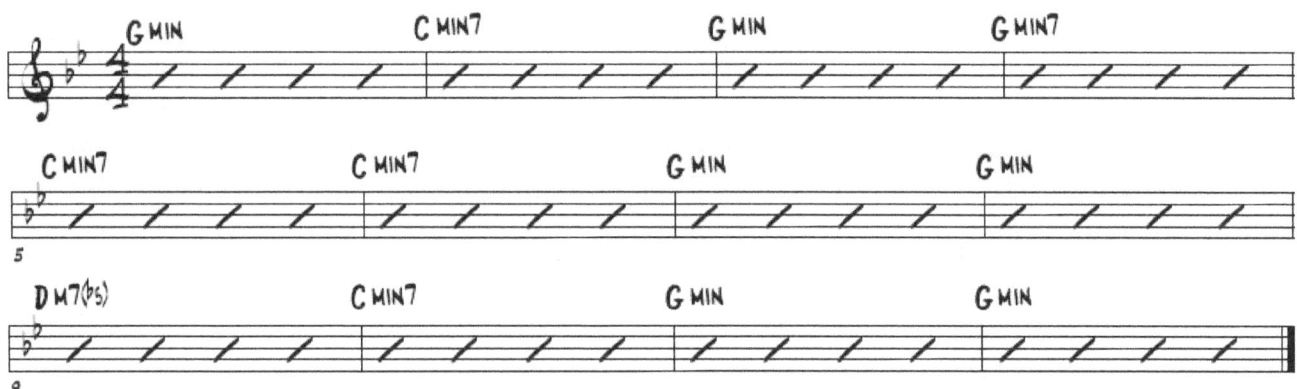

All the notes in all of the chords in a minor blues are members of the minor key's scale.

Non-blues Blues

Many tunes titled *blues* do not use the 12-bar blues changes. Many others use them for one refrain and other changes for others. Examples are: *Beale Street Blues, Blues in the Night*, and *Tishomingo Blues*. *St. Louis Blues* uses the usual 12-bar blues changes for two of its three refrains and a 16-bar minor key refrain for the other.

Chapter 15. Rhythm Changes

You learned the 1-6-2-5 changes in Chapter 13. The changes are often used as a *turnaround* (Chapter 16). Many old tunes use the 1-6-2-5 changes as a foundation for their refrains, among them are *Blue Moon*, *Heart and Soul*, *The Devil and the Deep Blue Sea*, and *I Got Rhythm*.

This chart contains *Rhythm Changes*, not a title unto itself but what we call the generic set of chord changes which are used in all those tunes and many more.

Be-boppers adapted the changes to *I Got Rhythm* in so many of their jazz tunes that the changes are identified as simply "Rhythm Changes," which they applied to such tunes as *Oleo*, *Cottontail*, and countless others. These changes were used for the theme song to the TV cartoon series, *The Flintstones*.

These are the vanilla changes. You can substitute the colorful ones.

Rhythm's refrain version of 1,6,2,5 uses a dominant 7 rather than a minor 7 for the 6 chord. This is a common substitution.

Rhythm substitutes a 3-minor 7 chord for the first chord of the second four measures, making it 3,6,2,5 changes, frequently used for refrains, bridges, and turnarounds (Chapter 16).

Bridge (3,6,2,5)

The bridge in Rhythm Changes—measures 17 through 24—is 3,6,2,5, which is a chord sequence comprised of dominant 7 chords with roots of the 3rd, 6th, 2nd, and 5th intervals, in the example above, D7, G7, C7, F7 for a B♭ key signature.

The chords in the bridge each occupy two measures and are all dominant 7s that walk the path of 4^{th}s to get back to the tonic chord in the last eight measures. The 3,6,2,5 changes are commonly called the "Sears Roebuck bridge" among musicians (Chapter 16).

AABA

Rhythm Changes are to an AABA tune, which is shorthand for a tune that has two eight-measure refrains which are called the A parts, followed by an eight-measure bridge called the B part, and ending with another eight-measure A part. Many tunes that you'll play will either follow that format or come close to it. AABA seems to be a "tin pan alley" innovation. Earlier tunes from the Great American Songbook favor a format with two 16-measure passages.

More contemporary jazz tunes can go off on harmonic and structural tangents, and more recent pop music styles such as punk, heavy metal, hip-hop, and others, don't seem to follow any patterns at all. Not a criticism, just how they are.

Tag

The original tune, *I Got Rhythm*, on which these changes are based, includes a *tag* at the end (Chapter 16), which is a closing passage not usually played with the chorus but in order to provide an orderly and dramatic ending to the tune. The chord chart above doesn't have that tag because most adaptations of Rhythm Changes in other tunes do not include a tag at the end but play the tune as a usual 32-measure AABA tune and maybe a tag at the end but not always. We'll talk more about tags in Chapter 16.

Chapter 16. Passages

Jazz and standard tunes often follow familiar patterns that musicians are accustomed to playing. These patterns employ *passages* of different kinds to comprise the tune.

The Chorus

The *chorus* is the outer passage, the main part of the tune, beginning to end, the part everyone is familiar with. The chorus contains and is surrounded by other passages.

Practice:

The following chord chart for the very old tune, *Ain't She Sweet*, is the chorus of that tune and it follows the AABA format.

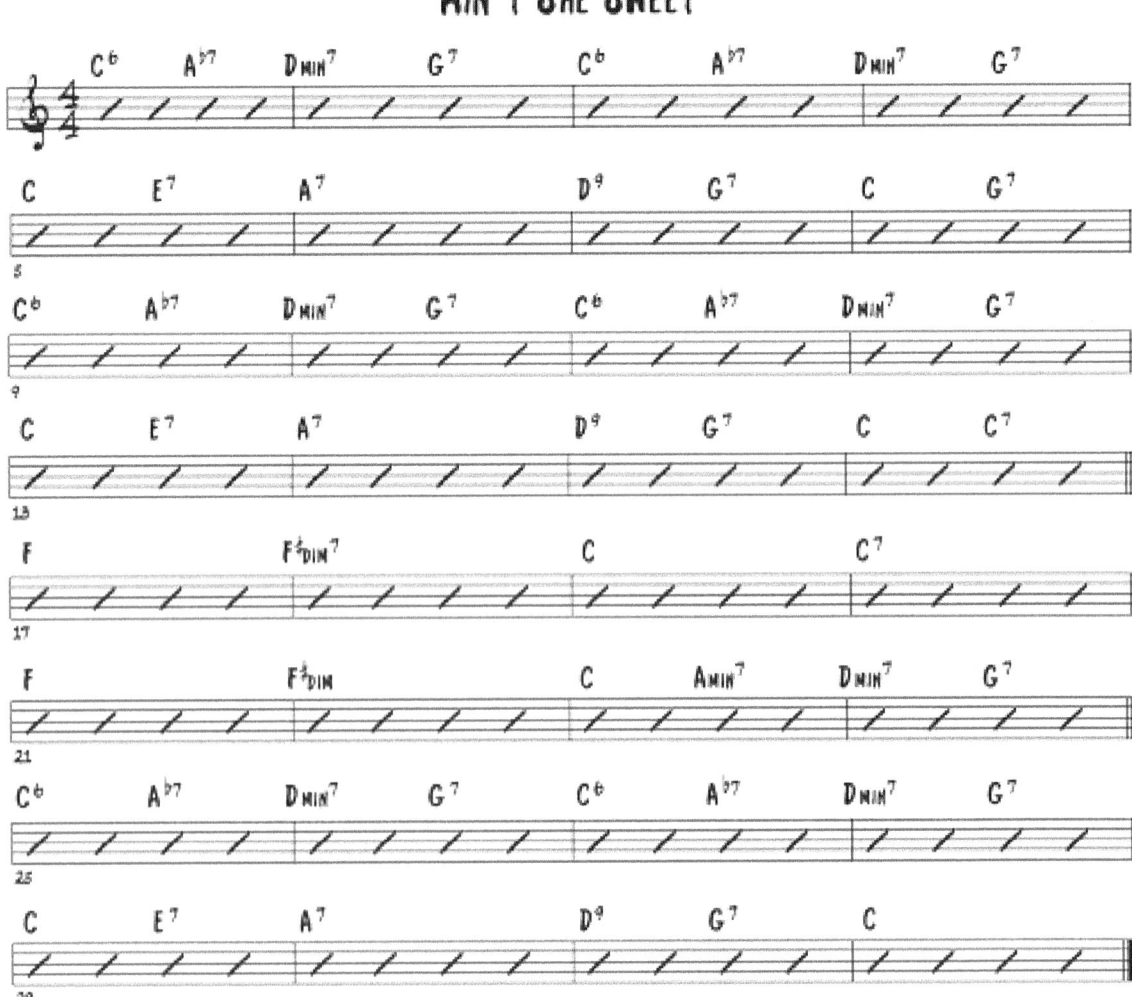

Intros

Jazz tunes often begin with an *intro* or "introduction," a musical passage that gets the tune started and sets up the first tonal center, which is usually the tune's key signature. It tells the musicians and singers when to come in. If you're reading from an arrangement, the intro is written for you and you just read it like you do the rest of the chart. If you're playing in a jam session or at a gig where you're playing a so-called *head* tune, one that everyone knows well enough to play by ear, the rhythm section plays the intro, and the leader tells the band how the intro goes by saying one of these:

"Start on top." This means there is to be no intro and the band begins playing the tune at its opening passage. Sometimes, in a noisy room, the leader uses sign language by tapping the top of his head with his palm. That also means "go back to the top" when you're improvising choruses.

"Four bars," or "eight bars." This tells the rhythm section to improvise an intro of four or eight bars, one that naturally segues into the tune's first refrain.

"Last four," or "last eight." The rhythm section is to play the last four or eight bars of the tune, which naturally seques into the top.

"Bring us in." If the tune is a ballad and there is a singer, the leader is telling the piano or guitar player to play a solo intro in a *rubato* tempo, which is free-style. The singer will come in where appropriate (you hope) and the leader will count the band in when the tempo is supposed to become a regular beat.

There are many changes for improvised intros, some well-known, others left to the player's fancy. Here is a generic intro in the key of C that can lead the chorus or verse into any tune that begins with a C chord.

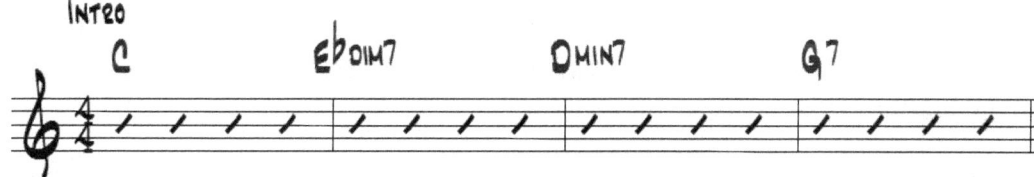

Sometimes the leader asks for an eight-bar intro. Players often use the last eight bars of the chorus as the intro. Here is such an intro that can be used with many standard tunes that begin with the IV chord.

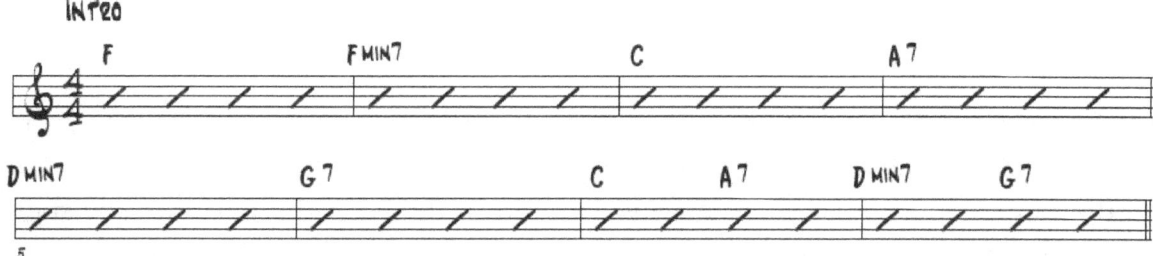

After playing six of the tune's last eight measures, the player inserts a 1-6-2-5 turnaround passage to bring in the top of the chorus.

This intro is generic. It fits many tunes.

If the band includes a piano player, it's best for the guitar player to sit out the intro and leave it to the piano player. This avoids harmonic clashes. If the leader wants a guitar intro, then the piano player usually sits out the intro.

The only rule—guideline, actually—for intros is that they end in a chord that resolves to the first chord of the tune's beginning refrain. If the tune is in C and starts on a C chord, the intro should end on a G7 chord. If the tune is in C and starts on an F chord—*After You've Gone*, for example—the intro should end on a C7 chord to resolve to the F in the first measure of the chorus.

Verses

Many tunes, particularly standards and show tunes, have a *verse*, which is a musical preface to the tune's chorus. Bands leave the verse out—not everyone knows the verse. To play or not to play the verse is a bandstand call. Sometimes I like verses more than the chorus itself. Vocalists like to sing verses because the lyrics, particularly in ballads, can be haunting as they offer a promise of a story to be told.

A nice verse can lead to a surprise for the audience because they're unfamiliar with it. You begin playing or singing the verse, often in rubato, and they don't know what tune is coming. When you reach the first chorus and they hear its familiar refrain, their tension is relaxed and they often break into applause.

Over the Rainbow has a beautiful verse that Judy Garland did not sing in the *Wizard of Oz* movie. When you play it, the audience is on the edge of their seats waiting to hear what's next. When they hear the first two notes, "Some-where..." they find out.

The verse that virtually everyone is familiar with is the verse to Hoagy Carmichael's *Stardust*. It's familiar because virtually every rendition of *Stardust* includes the verse, which is usually sung or played *rubato*, leading to the chorus in tempo.

> *Frank Sinatra recorded a version of Stardust in which the verse was the complete tune. He did not record the chorus. His explanation was that the Stardust verse is a beautiful song on its own. Legend has it that Carmichael was at first disturbed by Sinatra's omission of the chorus but changed his mind when he heard the recording.*

That could just be one of those *show biz* stories, typically more extraordinary than reality.

Turnarounds

A *turnaround* is a passage with which a player transitions between parts of the tune. Turnarounds usually and typically get you from the first A part to the second A part and from the third A part back to the top of the chorus. A turnaround is typically 1,6,2,5 if the next passage stays in the original tonal center and begins with that tonal center's tonic chord. Otherwise the turnaround uses a dominant 7 chord to resolve to the first chord of the next passage.

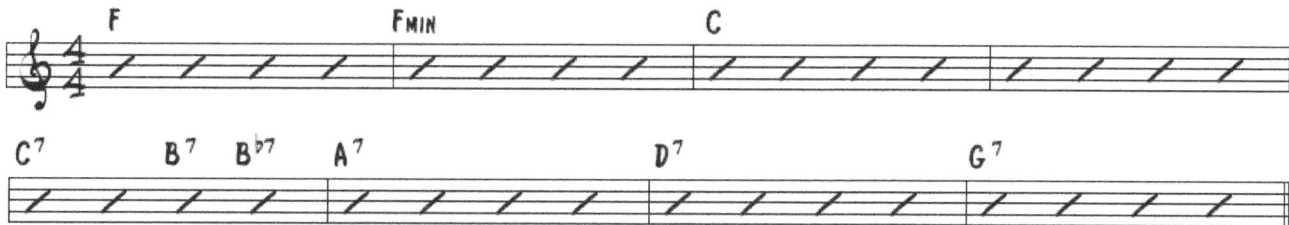

The last two measures of the intro shown a few paragraphs back is a typical 1-6-2-5 turnaround.

Bridge

The *bridge*, also called the *release*, is part B in an AABA tune. The bridge usually has different changes and melody from the A parts. There are various types of bridges, some with unique nicknames.

Some tunes don't have bridges. An old musician's joke addresses this variable in standard tunes.

> *A tourist gets lost in Louisville, Kentucky. He pulls over and hails a musician walking down the street.*
>
> *"Pardon me, sir," the tourist asks. "Where is the bridge to Indiana?"*
>
> *The musician replies, "There ain't no bridge to Indiana," and goes on his way.*

If you hum *Back Home Again in Indiana* or any of the be-bop tunes that are derived from the *Indiana* changes—*Donna Lee*, for example—you'll find that it consists of two sixteen-bar refrains and does not follow AABA at all. *Sweet Georgia Brown* goes without a bridge, too, as does its derivative jazz standard, *Dig*. The Les Paul, Mary Ford classic, *How High the Moon*, which donated its changes to Charlie Parker's *Ornithology*, has no bridge. And, *After You've Gone* has no bridge.

Generic IV Bridge

Many pop, country, rock, and folk AABA songs use these generic bridge changes. You'll play it so many times you can play it in your sleep. It begins on a IV chord and proceeds for 8 measures to return to the C chord that begins the third A part.

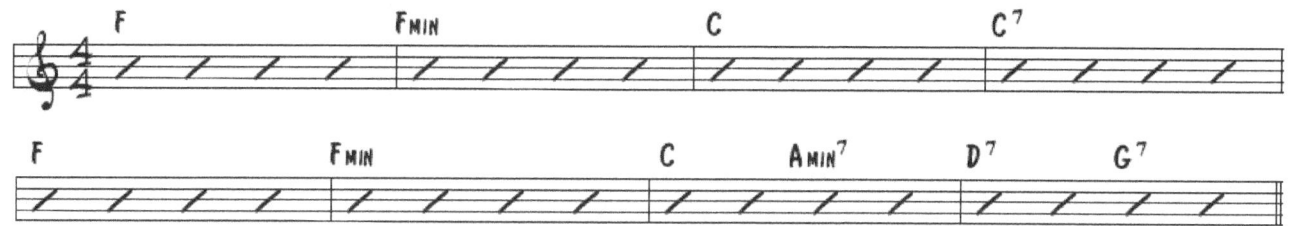

Some tunes use F#dim7 in the second and sixth measure of these bridges.

There are other generic bridge chord changes. You'll run into a lot of them as your playing experience expands.

Sears Roebuck Bridge

The *Sears Roebuck* bridge is an eight-bar chord sequence that many tunes use for their bridges, changing only the melody. The bridge is the same one you learned for the *Rhythm Changes* in Chapter 15. It uses a four chord progression with each chord getting eight beats or two measures. Here's that bridge again.

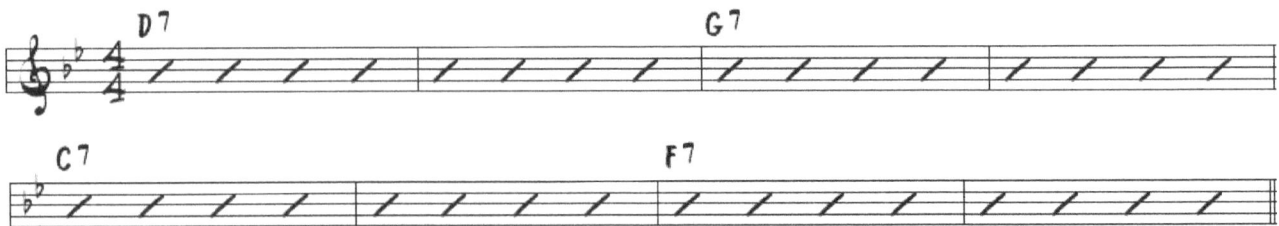

It is not unusual for musicians to expand these changes to make them more interesting. They might, for example, precede each of the dominant 7 chords with the minor 7 chord that resolves to it (Chapter 17).

Depending on your age, you might recognize the Sears Roebuck bridge from the old tune, *Five Foot Two*. The be-bop standards, *Cottontail, Oleo, Scrapple from the Apple, Perdido,* and many others use these changes in their bridges.

Montgomery Ward Bridge

The *Montgomery Ward* bridge is almost a cliché in old standards. Examples include *On the Sunny Side of the Street, Satin Doll,* and *Honeysuckle Rose,* and countless others. You'll find it in jazz tunes as well.

Montgomery Ward begins with the key signature's tonic chord in dominant 7 form. If you are playing in C, the first chord of the bridge is C7 as shown here.

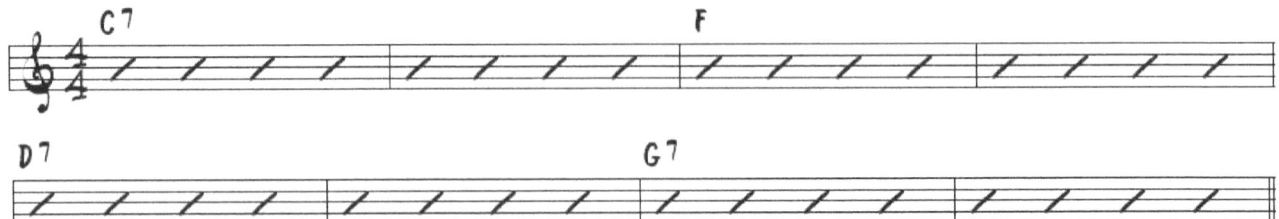

The bridge to *Honeysuckle Rose* teaches other lessons. It's a variation of Montgomery Ward that doesn't stay on the dominant 7 chords that walk it through the cycle. Instead, it uses passing chords that ascend from the current dominant 7 to the next one. In the key of F, the original, the bridge starts on the tonic dominant 7, F7. Instead of hanging there for two measures, it walks F to G to A♭ to A on its way to the B♭ resolution.

*teach yourself...*Jazz Piano Comping

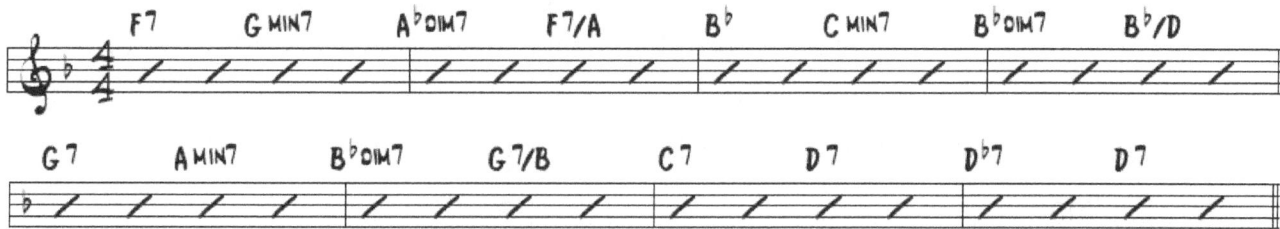

The chord voicings for the first three chords should put the root of each on the bottom. The fourth chord is an F7, but the bass note is A, which continues the ascending walking bass line. The second four chords follow the same pattern except beginning on B♭. The effect is a bass line beginning on F in an F7 chord and walking upwards to D in a B♭ chord. The next four chords go from G to B in a similar walk. The last four chords end the journey with a turnaround that gets the tune back to its A part, which begins on Gmin7.

If the band includes a bass player you might want to play other rootless voicings (Chapter 10) for these chords just to stay out of the way. If you're playing solo or in sole accompaniment of your own or someone else's vocals, you can play the bass line, and it will enhance the performance. You might even try playing the stride pattern with the bass note preceding the chordal part by half a beat. *Oomph-chuck, oomph-chuck...*

Endings

These are ways that you end a tune, not to be confused with band chart repeat ending notation (Chapter 20).

The end of a tune's performance is not necessarily part of the original composition but instead something to be determined by the arranger or the performers themselves.

Endings should bring the tune's performance to a climatic conclusion in a way that satisfies listeners and lets them know the tune has ended. In show tunes as performed theatrically, there are *big* endings and *little* endings, which means the tune goes out with a bang or kind of trails off. This depends on the mood of the story being told and the nature of the tune itself. *There's No Business Like Show Business* typically has a loud, flashy ending. *Send in the Clowns* might end in a more subdued manner.

A trend developed in the 1950s to have vocal recordings of pop tunes repeat the last phrase several times as the audio faded out. That worked for when we listened to records and the radio, but it always seemed awkward when artists lip-synced their hit recordings on TV. The audio faded out, but the vocalist didn't. They just stood there looking uncomfortable.

Short Endings

The next several endings use *rhythmic notation* (Chapter 19) in the last measure to indicate coming to the end. It might not always be that way. Some bands might sustain the last note. Get together and agree on how you'll do it. After you've played together for a while, you'll hear it coming.

Two-measure endings are so-called *short* endings. A short ending occupies the same number of measures as would the ending of any chorus in the tune that was not the *out* (last) chorus.

The endings themselves are two measures, the last two. The examples show the preceding two measures to show you how to fit the endings into the tune.

Generic Ending

A tune ending on its tonic for two measures often substitutes the tonic (I) and subdominant minor 7 (iv7) in the first of the two measures. Here's how that goes in the key of C.

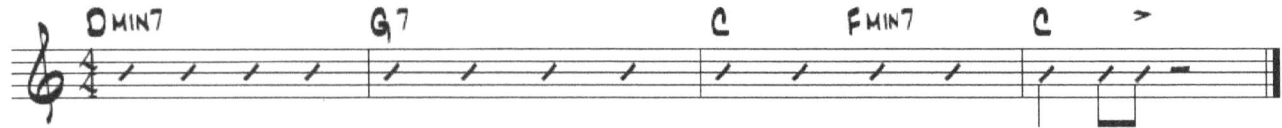

The ending shown here would be the last four measures in many tunes. It's common and if you are ready for it and listening, you'll play it automatically.

+Five Major Seven

A variation of the generic ending changes the two chords before the closing tonic chord to a major 7 chord of the augmented 5th interval, in this case in the key of C, an A♭ maj7.

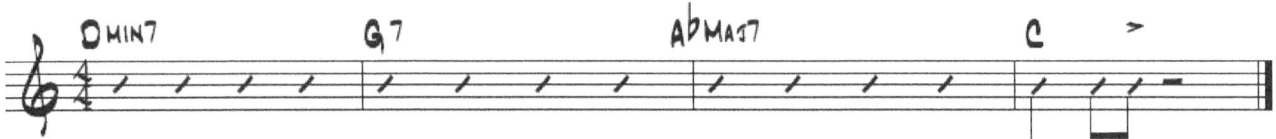

This ending works well with ballads.

A variation on that ending puts a D♭ maj7 in the second two beats of the next-to-last measure, giving the ending the properties of a tri-tone substitution resolution (Chapter 17).

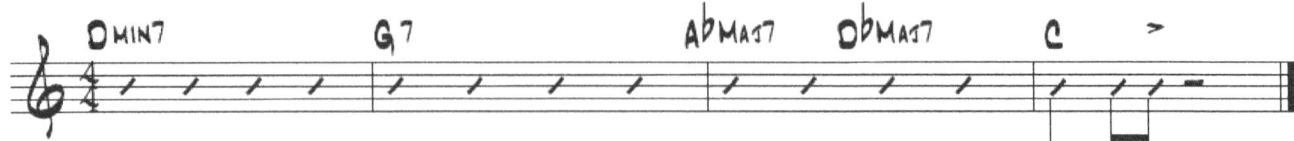

These two endings work because the last melody note, the root of the key signature's tonic chord, C in this example, is the third of the A♭ maj7 chord and the major 7th of the D♭ maj7 chord. You have to be careful when you use either of these. Make sure the vocalist or instrumentalist is going to sing or play a C (in this example). They have been known to warble a 3rd or 5th of the tonic chord, and sometimes a 9th, 6th, or even a flatted 5th just to sound hip. Any of these melodic substitutions can clash with your ending. Work it out in advance. Or wait until you hear the last melody note before you choose an ending.

Long Endings

The endings that follow are *long* endings. They take four measures.

Descending Bass

Here's a long ending in C that begins on the tonic and descends to the flat 7th and then proceeds downward chromatically two beats at a time until it gets to the V dominant 7 chord.

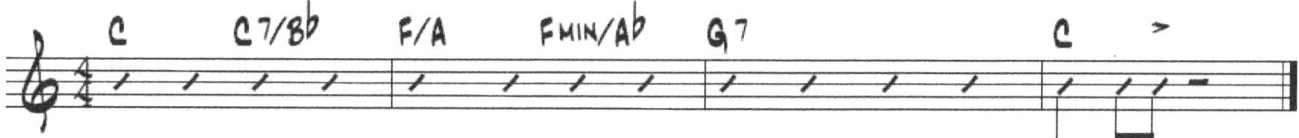

The bass line walks down from C to B♭ then A, A♭ and lands on G for a measure to resolve to the tonic C.

This example is of the ending itself. It replaces the last two measures of the tune.

Ascending Bass

Swing tunes often end with a four measure passage that walks the bass from the tonic up to the 5th, like this variation on the long ending.

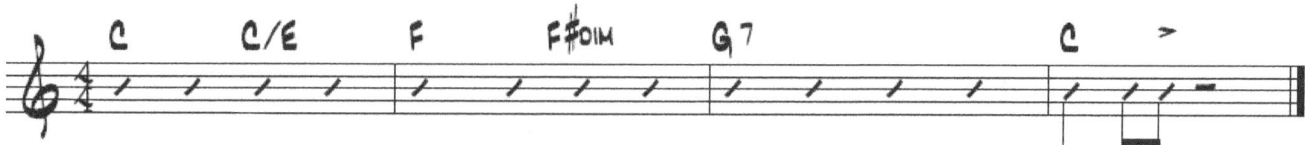

The bass line walks C, E, G, F#, G and finishes with C. The chord chart shows the chords you'd play to match the ending. For these long endings, we've omitted the two measures that lead into the ending. The C chord in the first measure shown above aligns with the last note in the tune, which a singer will typically hold until you get to that last measure.

Descending Bass from Flatted 5th

Bass players love this long ending. When they want you and the piano player to play it, they'll lean over and hit the first note with authority. I don't know why they do that but they always do. The descending notes begin on the flatted 5th of the signature key's tonic—F# in this case since we're in the key of C—and descend chromatically through F, E, E♭, D, D♭, and land on C, the root note of the signature key's tonic.

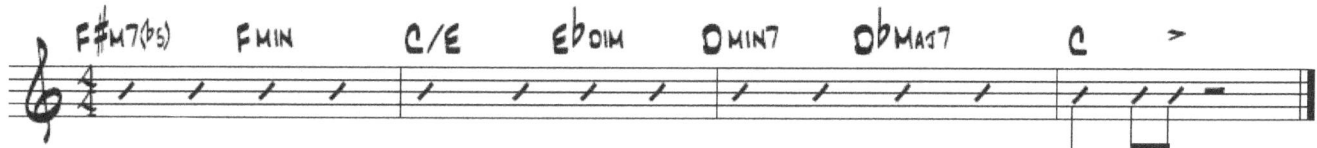

Be ready for this. You might be expecting to play the signature key's tonic chord. When you hear that big fat flatted 5th just go along with it.

Repeated Last Phrase

In this ending the last phrase of the tune, up to but not including the ending, is repeated twice.

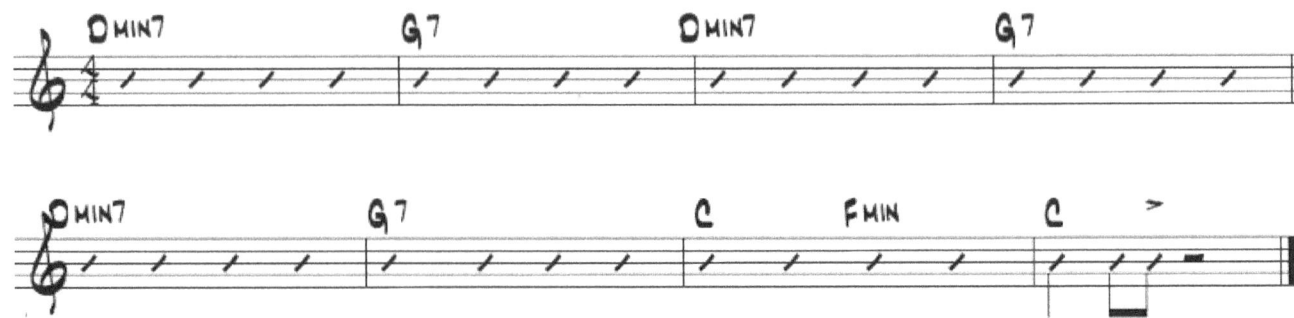

After the repeated phrase, the ending comes in. The ending after the repetitions can be long or short.

Tag

A *tag* is a special kind of long ending that extends the last chorus. It begins where the tune would normally end, with the last two measures. Instead of playing the short ending shown above, the tag substitutes a 3rd interval dominant 7 to a 5th interval dominant 7 progression. In C that would be E7 to A7. Then, it repeats the two measures ahead of the two it replaced, followed by whichever short or long ending you would otherwise have played. Here's the final A part of a tune in C with a tag and a short ending.

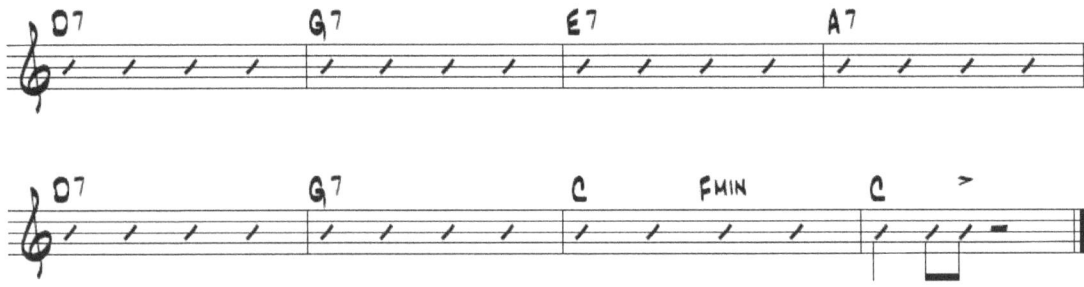

The third and fourth measures are the tag. You can see that if you delete the tag and the two measures that precede it, you get a tune with just a short ending.

You can add a long ending to a tag as well.

There are variations of how the tag gets from what would have been the tonic to the VI chord (A7 in this example). Sometimes you'll hit the tonic chord as a I7 and descend chromatically with dominant 7 chords to the VI.

Dixieland Ending

The typical Dixieland band ends most of its warhorse up-tempo tunes with a standard ending. It begins with a short ending just as we've seen above. Then the drums play a four-bar solo during which time the rest of the band lays out. Then the band repeats the last four measures of the tune:

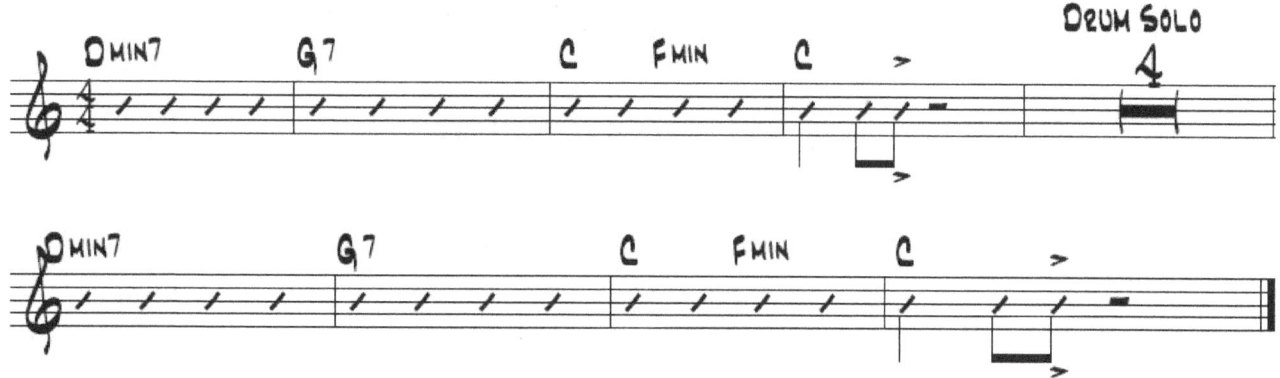

Sometimes the leader calls for a "last eight" ending, which means that after the tour bar drum solo, you play the chorus's final eight bars to the short ending.

One More Ending

Look at the last measure of all the endings in this discussion. They have the tonic chord hit with a rhythmic pattern of a quarter note and two eighth notes (Chapter 19) with the last note being short.

Now, consider this variation of that measure. Again we'll use the last four measures to make our point.

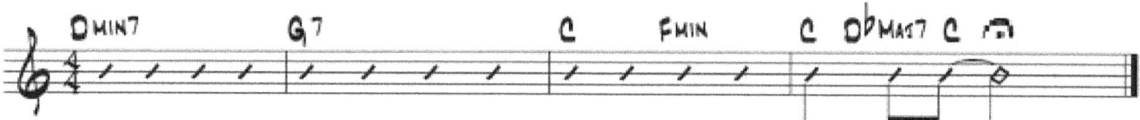

We're mainly interested in the last measure here. You can substitute it for the last measure on any of the endings in this chapter. The two-beat tonic chord and the hit on the third note of the other endings are replaced with a tonic chord, a tri-tone substitution of the V7 chord (D♭ maj7 in this example), and the tonic chord held sustained for the rest of the measure. That bird's eye symbol (a *fermata*, Chapter 20) above the note means to sustain (hold for an unspecified length of time) the chord. This idiom allows the vocalist or instrumentalist to do the same or to improvise an *obbligato* that wraps around the tonic's root and closes out the tune.

There's usually a drum hit when the sustained chord is done.

Chapter 17. Substitutions

Substitutions are chord changes, other than the original ones that a tune was published with but that fit nicely with the tune's melody. Some substitutions are referred to by jazz musicians as the "hip changes," and you are not regarded as "hip" if you don't play them. Don't let that kind of elitism worry you. As often as not, the original changes are every bit as pleasing and correct as the hip ones, while the hip changes themselves become clichés.

This chapter explains how to use chord sequence substitutions to reharmonize the strains in a tune.

This chapter does not provide comprehensive coverage of such substitutions. You learn only a few of them here to discover the potential for such reharmonizations.

You can skip all this and still play effective piano accompaniments by using standard changes. But I urge you to delve into it all. These are the harmonic enhancements that so-called *progressive jazz* players discovered in the middle of the 20th century and that have driven the advancement of jazz theories ever since.

If you're playing in a group, you have to coordinate these substitutions with the other players, particularly the piano and bass players. And you should learn to recognize them when you hear the other players use them, a collaboration that often comes intuitively after you've been working together for a while.

Just because a substitution is hip doesn't mean you should use it every time. Certainly you coordinate chord changes for a recording session. Recordings are permanent, and their clams (musical mistakes) and train wrecks can never be forgotten. On the bandstand, particularly in jams, just listen and don't go off on a tangent with some off-the-wall substitution that nobody ever heard of.

This chapter touches on only a few such substitutions, the blues variations and tri-tone substitutions being the most prevalent.

*teach yourself...*Jazz Piano Comping

The Blues Redux

Chapter 14 taught you the fundamental chord changes for the twelve-bar blues. Now, you'll learn some alternative blues changes that have come into widespread use among jazz musicians. We'll keep it all in the key of G.

For review and reference, here are the basic blues changes you learned in Chapter 14:

Nothing's changed about the blues since then, but some things are about to.

Blues Substitution #1 (de facto)

The first set of substitutions is common and is shown here. Unless you are in a rock band, chances are the bass player will play these changes without giving it a second thought. These have become the *de facto* standard changes for jazz-oriented blues.

Practice:

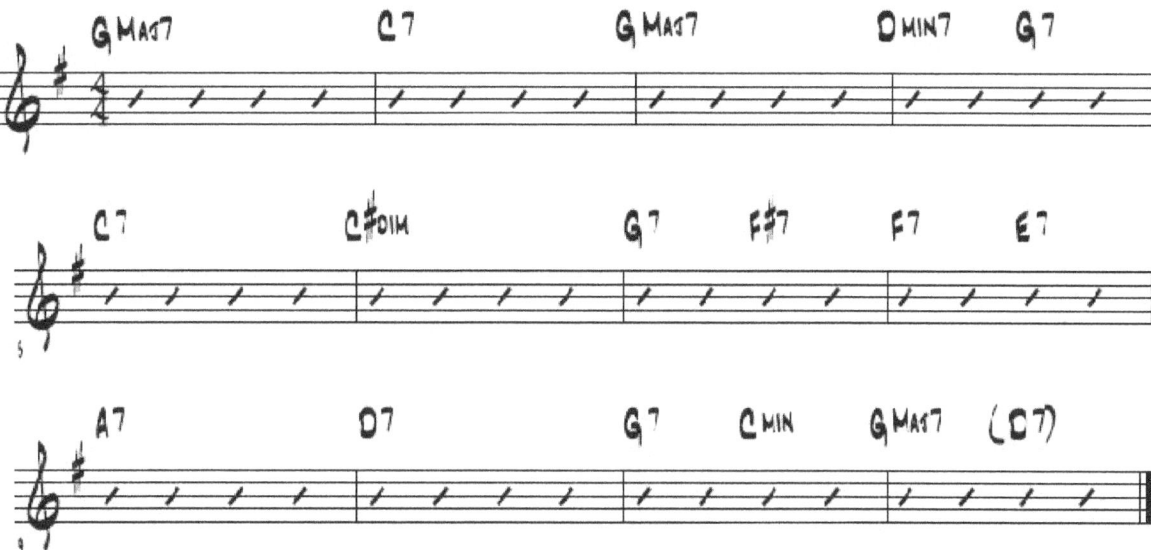

The first change you see when comparing these blues to those in the original changes is that the first chord is Gmaj7. Then, in measure 4, the G7 is replaced with Dmin7 G7. This is a common substitution for many dominant seven chords, which this chapter discusses in **Preceding Minor 7**. The C7 in measure 6 is replaced with a C#dim chord. Next, beginning in measure 7, the G7 chord begins a downward chromatic progression of F#7, F7, to land on E7. Finally, in measure 9, A7 resolves to D7 in measure 10, which resolves to G7 in measure 11. If this is the end of the performance—the last chorus—the final D7 is left out. Otherwise it leads back to measure 1 for the next chorus.

Blues Substitution #2 (Bird changes)

The second substitution for the blues employs the well-known "Bird" changes, named after Charlie Parker, who was known to take harmonic liberties with the tunes he played.

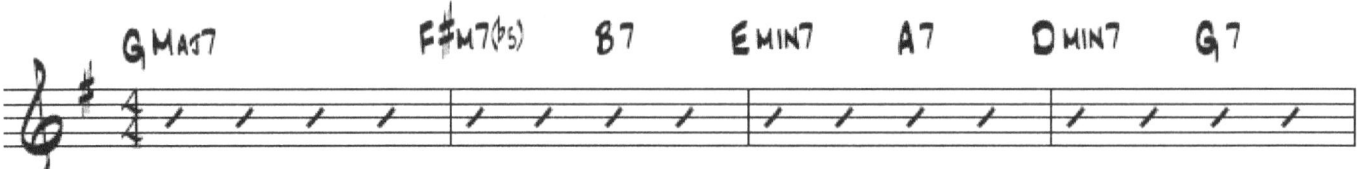

We need look only at the first four measures for this substitution. The rest of the changes are standard blues. One thing most blues changes have in common is that they begin with the tonic in measure one (Gmaj7 in this case) and resolve to the tonic dominant 7 in measure 4 (G7 in this case). The various substitutions or variations have to do with how the changes get there. In this substitution, the second measure moves down a half tone from the tonic and plays three measures of the cycle of 4^{th}s, two beats to the chord. It varies between minor 7 and dominant 7 as it travels the cycle, ending on the G7 which was the objective from the start.

There are many other blues substitutions. If you know these two in all the jazz keys, you are well prepared to hold forth at the local jam. You'll encounter others in band and chord charts, and lead sheets as you expand your jazz repertoire. Each time you find a new one, put it to use and make it part of your jazz vocabulary.

Exercise:
Play the blues with both substitutions in G over and over. Use the backing tracks (Appendix B). Get other musicians to jam with you.

Exercise:
Transpose the blues to B♭, C, E♭ and F. Jam on those changes too.

Tri-tone Substitution

The *tri-tone substitution* is the best known and most often used jazz substitution. It's a hip-sounding substitution of one chord where a different one is expected, specifically, of the chord that is three tones away from the original one.

What's a *tri-tone*? It's what its name implies. It's an interval three full tones away. For example, the tri-tone of C is F#. Count the whole tone intervals between the two. C, D, E, F#. You move upward three whole tones—a tri-tone—to get there. If you move downward, C, B♭, A♭, F#, it's the same number of tones.

It follows that since C's tri-tone is F#, F#'s tri-tone is C. The same relationship exists between all six tri-tone pairs in the twelve-tone scale. Here they are:

C, F#

D♭, G

D, A♭

E♭, A

E, B♭

F, B

Now, consider the harmonic properties of a dominant 7 chord. C7, for example, resolves to F in the cycle of 5ths/4ths (Chapter 11). It is harmonically pleasing to allow F# to resolve to F as well, since F is a half step down.

Exercise:

Play these chords. C7, F and then F#7, F.

You'll hear the similarity. Both dominant 7 chords, tri-tones of each other, readily resolve to the same major chord.

It then follows that if Gmin7, C7, F sounds good, you can insert F#'s preceding minor 7 chord in the substitution, by playing D♭min7, F#7, F. Why does this work? Because D♭ and G are tri-tones to one another, and D♭min7 resolves to F#7.

The D♭min7 chord can also be named C#min7 and many experts might insist that it should be.

The tri-tone has other applications for hip substitutions. Players tend to call it the *flatted 5th* substitution because tri-tones are also the flatted 5ths of each other. We'll explore some of that next.

Flatted 5th Descent

Like the tri-tone substitution for dominant 7 chords, the flatted 5th descent is widely known and popular among musicians. It's often used as an ending (Chapter 16), but it works well at phrases that normally begin on the tonic and proceed one way or another to the ii chord. Consider many pop standards with A part beginnings harmonized this way to get from the tonic to the V7 chord in four measures:

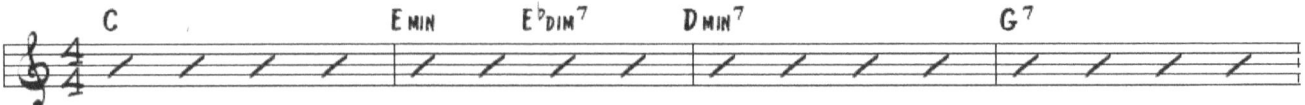

Here's the same progression but with the flatted 5th descent substituted in the first measure:

This version of the flatted 5th descent substitution substitutes itself for the tonic chord rather than for a dominant 7, and its tri-tone chord is half-diminished to accommodate the melody.

Alternative Reharmonizations

These are the hip changes that musicians often substitute for the originals. In some cases, the hip changes have become *de facto* standard changes, and the original ones are forgotten or at least discarded. Several of Hoagy Carmichael's tunes—*Skylark*, *Stardust*, and *Georgia on my Mind*, for example—have been reharmonized by jazz players. If you could ask them—if they were still alive—they'd say they "fixed" the tunes.

Often, a reharmonization happened because sheet music publishers of yore dumbed down piano arrangements to make them easier for amateur pianists, guitarists and ukulele strummers. The easy chords weren't always the best choices, and the jazz players were quick to correct the problem.

We'll look at passages from two ballads in which the changes have been rewritten for a more pleasing—to the jazz player's ear—sound. You can compare the originals with the updated versions to see which you prefer. As with most substitutions, you should coordinate their choice with the other players in your ensemble.

Someone to Watch Over Me

George Gershwin wrote *Someone to Watch Over Me* in 1926 and it became a timeless standard recorded by pop and jazz musicians countless times.

teach yourself...Jazz Piano Comping

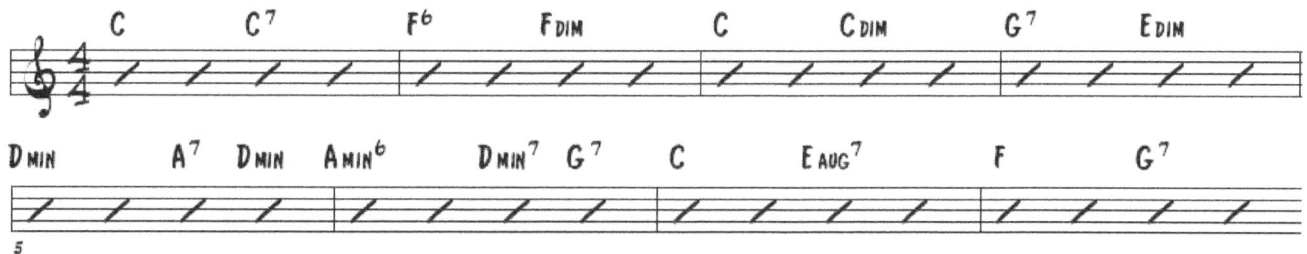

In the 1950s, pianist Art Tatum recorded *Someone to Watch Over Me* and introduced harmonic substitutions that essentially redefined the tune. Musicians have been using these alternative changes ever since.

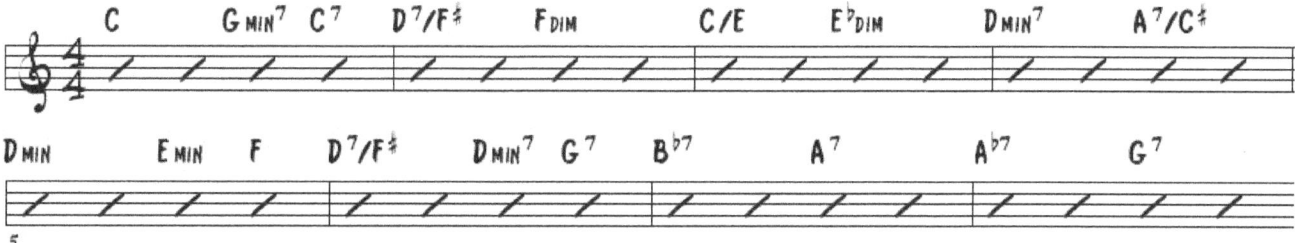

Tatum's changes are a study in the use of harmonic substitutions to insert lines—chromatic descents and ascents—as counter melodies. In the second measure he begins with an F# that then descends chromatically over the next two measures to land on the C# that is the 3rd of the A7 chord. Then, in the fifth measure, he heads back up the chromatic scale from D to F# on the first beat in measure 6. After that he ends the first eight measures with a substitution for the 1-6-2-5 turnaround (Chapter 16) with another chromatic descent from B♭ to G.

Tatum's interpretation also changes how the bridge is harmonized. I'll leave that to you to research.

I Can't Get Started With You

This is the original version of *I Can't Get Started With You* as penned by Vernon Duke. It has been recorded countless times with these changes as the preferred ones.

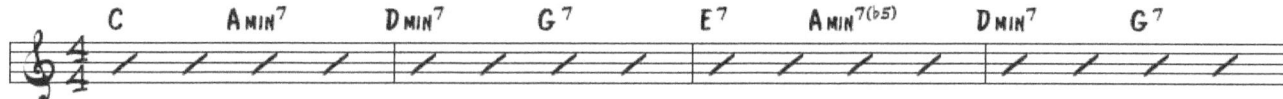

Sometime during the be-bop era, someone crafted these alternative changes, and they have become the ones of choice by many jazz musicians.

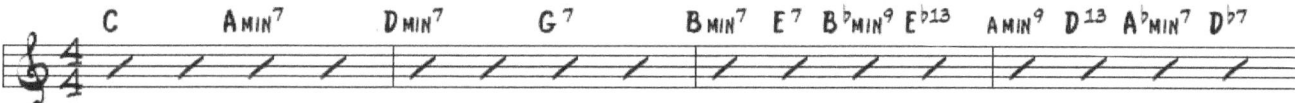

The substitution runs a two-chord minor 7 to dominant 7 sequence descending one-half tone at a time. The two final chords in that descent, A♭min7 to D♭7, are the tri-tone substitution for the original version's G7, both of which resolve to the C in the next measure (not shown here).

PART V The Charts

Are you ready to read some music? Don't know how? Don't worry, you don't have to learn everything there is to know about scores. But there are some basics that will come in handy when you get together with other musicians and somebody pulls out an arrangement or a fake book. And, of course, reading is a required skill when you play in a big band. This Part explains what you'll need in order to get started.

Chapter 18. Chord Charts

We've seen chord charts earlier as we learned about parts of the tunes. Now, we'll learn about the charts themselves. Don't skip this chapter. You are assumed in the next two chapters to know the concepts and chart components explained here. If you think you already know them, read it anyway so we're speaking the same language later.

To begin, here is the complete chord chart for the old jazz standard, *After You've Gone*.

teach yourself...Jazz Piano Comping

After You've Gone was originally written and played in two-beat, which was the popular dance idiom in 1918 when it was written and first became popular. Jazz players adopted it, sped it up, doubled its time to four-beat, and it became a standard.

This chart uses *slash* notation, except for the last measure which uses *rhythmic* notation (Chapter 19). You might be given a similar chart with melody notes in keyboard notation. That would be a lead sheet, and, unless you're playing a melodic solo (Chapter 22), you can ignore the notes and assume slash notation, four beats to the measure.

The chords are simple—you've already seen some of them in this book.

The chart shown here is the complete tune, one chorus. It does not include intros, turnarounds, endings, or any other kind of additional passages (Chapter 16) other than what are part of the tune itself. You will be expected to play from this chart with as many choruses as the performance and the configuration of your group demands. If it's a combo, you'll play the head once or twice, then you will accompany solos by the individual players, which might include you if you are up to it. The only time you lay out completely is during a drum solo or some other special head arrangement called out at the time. For example, a sax player might want to play with bass only with the rest of the rhythm section laying out.

The chart is the tune itself. How you play it, how many choruses, and so on, are specified at the moment. The chart simply tells you what chords to play during each chorus.

You might be expected to provide a dominant 7 chord in the last measure to resolve back to the top for each of the choruses except the last one. You might be expected to play a canned ending (Chapter 16) at the end of the last chorus.

After You've Gone begins on the IV chord instead of the tonic, so your chord getting back to the top would be the I chord, B♭7 in this case.

Whatever is expected of you, this chart is not an arrangement; it's not even a road map. All of that exists in the heads of the players at the time of the performance.

Title

The title is at the top of the chart. You recognize that.

Staves

Each row of five horizontal lines is a *staff*. Each staff section divided by vertical lines is a *measure*, also called a *bar*. The vertical lines are *barlines*. The chord symbols are above the staves (plural of staff) they are to be played in. Those are the chord names you learned about in Chapter 3.

This chart consists of ten staves of four measures each. Most chord charts will be thirty-two measures. *After You've Gone* does not follow the AABA format and thus has forty measures. Each measure has four beats as you can see.

Clef Sign

That funny looking backward S symbol at the beginning of each staff tells the player that they should read the *treble clef*. Don't worry about that if you don't know what it means. Clefs are meaningless in a chord chart because you can play chords with either or both hands anywhere on the keyboard.

Key Signature

The cluster of two little ♭ symbols to the right of the clef sign in the first staff is the *key signature*. It tells you what key the tune is in, in this case, B♭. Again, it's helpful to know that, but it isn't absolutely necessary. You're given all the chord symbols, and the key signature should not affect how you play them. It will, however, affect how you play *fills* (Chapter 21).

Here are the key signatures you can expect to encounter as you read small and big band charts.

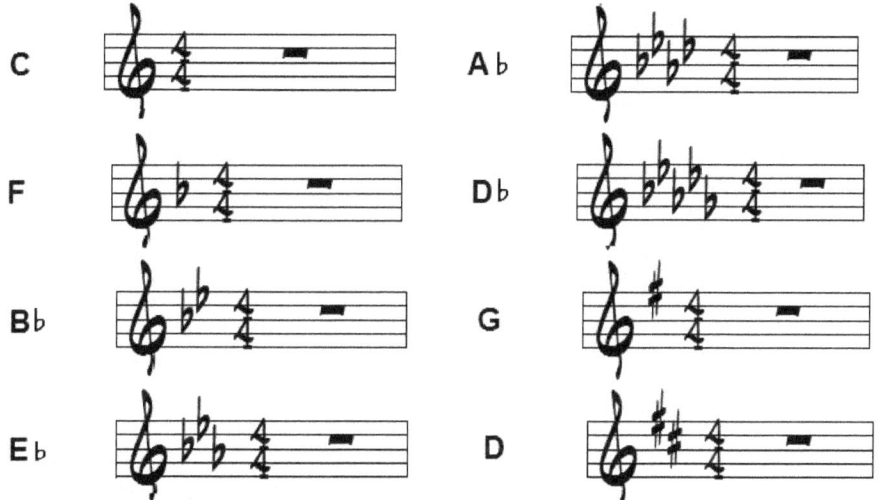

There are others, of course, but these are the standard jazz keys and the keys that standard tunes were originally published in sheet music. The relative minor keys share these signatures. Not many charts are written in D, although the standards *Wave* and *I'm Getting Sentimental Over You* are. The latter is often transposed to B♭ to make it easier for the players.

Time Signature

The 4 over 4 symbol to the right of the key signature is the *time signature*. The top 4 means that there are four beats to the measure. The lower 4 specifies that each quarter note gets a beat, something that you don't need to worry about when reading chord sheets. You'll need to know it later. The time signature does not repeat on successive staves. It will, however, be included if the time changes, something that doesn't happen in mainstream jazz (or shouldn't).

Note that a waltz will specify 3 over 4, meaning three beats to the measure in which case you should expect each measure to have three instead of four slashes.

There are other time signatures. *Take Five* is five beats to the measure. Other than for that one, unless you are playing Dave Brubeck standards, you won't have to worry about them. If you are called upon to read a chord chart on *Take Five* expect five slashes and play them like 1-2-3-1-2.

Measures

The tiny digits under the first measure of each staff is the measure number, which you use to discuss the chart with other players.

"Hey, pops, you played the wrong change at measure 22."

Note that measures 16 and 24 have a double vertical line separating them from their next measure. This tells you, in this case, where a new passage (Chapter 16) begins and ends. That's handy for when you get lost, but not all charts use the convention. In AABA tunes, the double lines identify where the B part, the bridge, begins and ends.

Tempo

Note that the chart has a tempo indication above the first staff's first measure. That indication specifies how many beats to the minute or it might simply say something meaningful about the tune: "slow," "medium," and so on. Don't worry about it. If you know the tune, you'll know how fast or slow it should be played. Otherwise, the leader or the vocalist or instrumentalist you are accompanying will kick off the tempo.

Chapter 19. Rhythmic Notation

Rhythmic notation uses the chord chart format but adds note-like symbols to describe rhythmic patterns the rhythm section is expected to play. This depiction is common in big band charts. You'll see the same rhythmic patterns on the drum and guitar parts and often the trumpet parts too, although they'll have specific notes to play. We'll discuss this further in Chapter 20.

Look back at the *After You've Gone* chord chart in Chapter 18, which is mostly slash notation. The following is a different old song in traditional AABA format that also uses slash notation but with places where rhythms are specified.

I wrote this song when I was a teenager. My best friend sang it in a high school talent show to my accompaniment. I dedicated it to a girl I was interested in. She was embarrassed at being called out publicly by the school nerd and never spoke to me again.

Pay attention to measures 7 and 8, 15 and 16, 24, and 32. All the other measures use slash notation, which means you typically play four to the bar. But those measures have note-like symbols and rests. Each symbol represents a beat, a portion of a beat, or more than one beat. How much depends on the note symbol's shape.

There's more to rhythmic notation than you will learn here, but this introduction will get you started. If you are playing in a session where precision is required, the other players will correct you if you mess something up. Eventually with experience, you'll reach a point where when you look at a measure or several measures of rhythmic notation, you know how the rhythms work.

This chart is in 4/4 time, which means there are four beats to each measure and a quarter note gets a beat. That's all you need to know about time signatures for now. As a jazz player you will sometimes play in 3/4 time and very rarely in 5/4 time.

The following chart specifies the shape and beat value of each of the rhythmic notation note and rest symbols. It gets a lot deeper than this for melodic and harmonic parts, but these are about all you'll see in slash and rhythmic notation accompaniment charts.

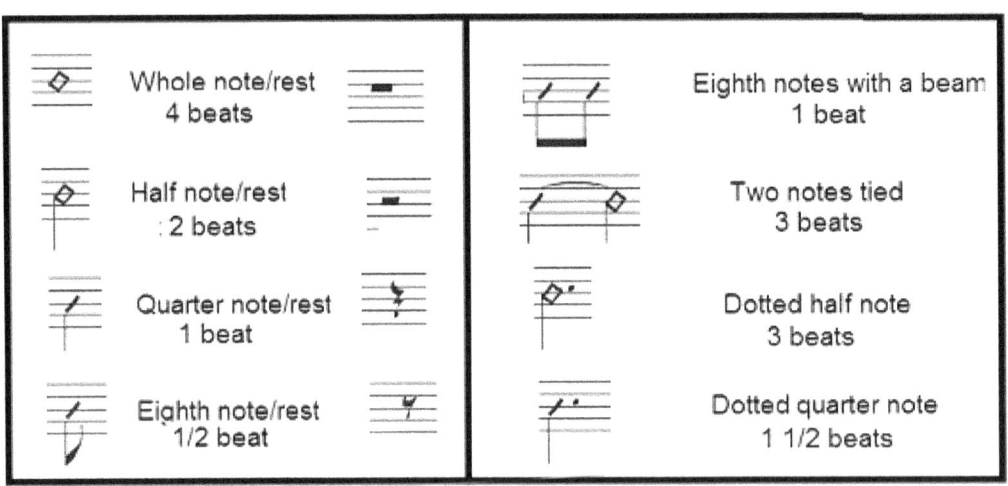

To put this notation into context, you have to start at the beginning. We won't do that here; there are many tutorials available to teach you to read music. For now, consider this small example.

Count this off following the beat numbers under the staff. Think, *one and two and three and four* for each measure

The first note gets two beats. The second and third notes get one beat each. That's the first measure.

The first note in the second measure is an eighth note which gets a half beat. That means the second note in that measure starts a half-beat ahead of the second beat on the first "and" and is a quarter note that lasts the value of a beat, so it lasts until the second half of the second beat on the second "and".

The third note in the second measure is an eighth note, so the first three notes in the second measure equal two beats although only the first one is sounded on a beat. The last note in that measure is another half note that finishes the measure.

Got all that? Great. Here's a trick. Read the notation, speaking the lyrics in a meter that matches the rhythms.

"Hey, you there, who parked the car?"

The next time you see an eighth-quarter-eighth sequence of notes followed by another note, "who parked the car" will pop into your head. Eventually all the rhythmic patterns you'll ever see you will have seen countless times, and you'll know what they sound like without having to hear them first.

This small treatment is just an introduction, an overview, a sneak preview of reading music. To sight read a full chart takes lots of practice. Imagine having to combine that with note values to play melodies and harmonies. That's what your colleagues in the big bands have to do. Of course, you have to combine these beat values with the chord symbols above them, not shown in the example, but that are on all the chord charts.

Better get started.

Chapter 20. Big Band Charts

Reading band charts is another of those skills that takes lots of practice to master. It gets easier as you progress. If you play in a big band, you'll get to read a fixed set of arrangements, the band's standards. Virtually every big band plays *In the Mood*, for example. Your band will have its own set of other standard tunes as well, usually favorites that your audiences recognize and like to dance to.

From reading those arrangements, you'll come to recognize the notations that tell you what to play and when. Eventually you'll be able to sight-read charts you've never seen before.

That's your goal as a big band piano player. Studio playing needs musicians who can read the charts on sight without consuming expensive studio time and the time of the other musicians learning what's on the chart. I recommend finding a local community big band that needs a piano player, maybe just a relief player. If you can do everything this book teaches, they'll be looking for you.

This chapter is an overview. If you run into notation that isn't explained—and there is a lot more to it than we show here—ask one of your fellow musicians about it. To understand this discussion, you must already know what is presented in Chapters 18 and 19. A review of those chapters might be helpful before you get into this one.

You have two kinds of notational symbols to watch for besides the ones that specify chords and rhythms. These two categories are *navigation* and *interpretation* chart symbols, also called *markings*.

The chart for *A Place Called Nowhere*, shown below, contains elements you'll need to understand on the piano part for big band arrangements. Once you have them under your belt, you'll be ready to take on the real thing.

It might look cryptic and esoteric and it is. But you'll learn what it all means with practice.

The most frequent problem experienced by reading newcomers is keeping their place in the chart and not getting lost.

You already learned to read simple chord charts (Chapters 18 and 19) that lay down the changes and rhythmic patterns for one chorus of a tune. Big band charts have all that plus other markings that tell you when to play what, where to go next on the chart, and small subtleties, such as dynamic and expression markings.

What Does the Leader Want?

There is more than one way to comp in a big band, and what is expected of you will vary from band to band, depending on what the leader wants to hear. Some band leaders want to hear a lot of piano fills even during the instrumental passages. Others want to hear virtually no piano at all; to them, the piano is an invisible and silent entity in the band unless the arrangement calls for specific notes to be played. These leaders want you to play nothing but chords in time with the chart, varying rhythmic patterns only when the piano chart calls for it.

It's up to you to figure out what kind of leader you're working for. Some will tell you if they want something different. Others will ignore you and you won't be called again to play for that leader.

> *I was playing piano in the Harry James ghost band under the leadership of the late, great trumpet player Art Depew. It was our first rehearsal and I was playing a lot of accompaniment. Art stopped the tune and said, "Less is more, Al. Just keep time" I got the message.*

When in doubt, ask the bass player what the leader prefers in piano accompaniment. Or you might ask the leader. That could lessen your esteem in that leader's eyes, though. They all think the way they like it is the right way, the only way, and if you don't know it, they need to hire someone else.

I always ask the bass player first.

*teach yourself...*Jazz Piano Comping

A Chart to Study

This chapter gives an overview of each of the markings on such charts. We use an arrangement of a tune I wrote called *A Place Called Nowhere*. You'll find a backing track for the tune at http://www.alstevens.com/jazzpianocomping so you can hear the lyrics and melody.

It might be helpful to print this chart so you can highlight the various elements as we discuss them. If you cannot print from this book, you can download a PDF of the chart from

http://www.alstevens.com/jazzpianocomping/.

Now let's look at *A Place Called Nowhere* piece by piece.

Rehearsal Numbers

There are two uppercase letters inside circles, one at measure 5 and the other at measure 13. These are called *rehearsal numbers* even though they aren't really numerical digits. Some arrangements will indeed have numbers. Some will be boxed rather than in circles. Some leaders will say "circle one," "circle two," and so on, whether they're in boxes, circles, or whatever. Their purpose is to provide ways to address specific locations in the arrangement when you and the other players discuss it. They have no bearing on the chart's playing or your navigation of it.

teach yourself...Jazz Piano Comping

Navigation

Navigation is important to any journey. It keeps you from getting lost. That's why the navigation markings on an arrangement are often called a *road map*.

When I see a big band chart for the first time, my first task is to eyeball it beginning to end, making a mental note of where the navigational markings are so that when I get to a mark that jumps the arrangement to another place in the chart, maybe several pages away, forward or backward, I am not surprised. I already know where that destination is on the chart.

A yellow highlighting pen is helpful, but get permission first. The band's librarian might not want you marking up the pages.

> *I was pianist with the Tommy Dorsey Orchestra for a couple years, and we used the same paper chart copies that the original band used in the 1930s, 40s, and 50s. They had an antique value to my traditional thinking, so, out of respect for their antiquity, I used small Post-it notes stuck to the margins to mark where things were.*

The chart consists of a four-measure intro (Chapter 16), the chorus played twice, and a tag with a long ending (Chapter 16). Finding your way from the beginning to the end of the arrangement requires you to read and correctly interpret the navigation markings.

This chart has measure numbers at the beginning of each staff. We can use them to reference the markings.

Repeat Signs

These two markings, the first at measure 5 and the second at measure 20, are left and right *repeat signs* that mark a passage that is to be played more than once.

The first time you encounter the left repeat sign, you pass it by. Don't ignore it, though. Remember where it is, because when you come to the right repeat sign, you return to the measure that follows the left repeat sign, and in a complex big band chart, that can be several pages back. If there is no left repeat sign, you return to the beginning of the passage marked by the nearest double bar, or if there is no double bar, the beginning of the arrangement.

Endings

These markings mark the endings of repeated passages. You play the first ending, the one numbered 1 at measure 17, the first time you play the passage. When you reach the right repeat sign at measure 20, you return to the left repeat sign at measure 5 and play the passage a second time. This time, when you get to the first ending at measure 17, you jump over it to the second ending at measure 21 and play that.

teach yourself...Jazz Piano Comping

This arrangement uses only two endings for its one repeated passage, but there can be endings, 3, 4, and so on, and there can be multiple repeated passages and endings in an arrangement.

Segno

Segno is Italian for *sign*. Most musicians call it by its English name.

The sign marks a place in the chart where the arrangement will return to resume playing. In the chart above, it's at measure 5 along with the rehearsal number A and the left repeat sign. Don't confuse the two signs. The left repeat sign needs a right repeat sign paired with it to tell you when to return, and, of course, they need to be in logical proximity to one another so there's no question about where to return to. The sign, however can be returned to from anywhere later in the arrangement as explained next in the discussion of **D.S. al Coda**.

D.S. al Coda

The **D.S. al Coda** marking (measure 24) directs you to return to the sign (measure 5) and proceed playing until you arrive at the *Coda* marking (measure 22).

D.C. al Coda

The **D.C. al Coda** marking (not on the example chart) directs you to return to the beginning of the arrangement, the very first measure.

Coda

The *Coda* marking at measure 22 tells you to complete that measure and jump to what is called the *Coda*, which begins at measure 25.

You make the jump only if you are at the coda sign following the D.S. al Coda or D.C. al Coda. Otherwise, you passed it by, although you should take note of where it is for the next time through.

Sometimes, the first *Coda* marking is replaced with text that says, *to Coda*.

The second *Coda* (measure 25 in the example) marks the beginning of the last passage in the arrangement. Most times.

Repeated Measures

Measure 28 contains a marking that tells you to repeat the previous measure.

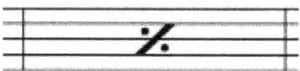

You would play the chord and rhythms in measure 27 a second time.

Multimeasure Rests

Measures 1 through 4 are represented by this marking:

This is a *multimeasure rest*. You will lay out (rest, remain tacit) for the number of measures noted in the marking, four in this case. Just sit quietly and count.

Speaking of that, it is considered bad form to count in such a visible manner that the audience can tell that's what you're doing. It's okay to tap your foot and count mentally, but don't mouth the words of the numbers you are counting. "***One***, *two, three, four,* ***two****, two three, four...*" Don't do that. It identifies you as an amateur. Don't count on your fingers, either.

Interpretation

Up to now, you've learned how to identify and form your chords, when to play them, and how to find your way around a chart. Now, you'll get into the more subtle, the more sensitive aspects of reading. Every piece of music is subject to the interpretation of the musician with respect to tempo, volume, attack, and so on. But arrangements have written clues as to how the arranger wants you to interpret the work, to insert his or her own interpretation, and to keep all the musicians in the ensemble on the same track.

These markings specify the arranger's intentions with respect to dynamics and articulation.

Dynamics

The *dynamics* markings of a musical note, measure, passage, and the tune itself denote how loudly or softly you are to play at various places in the performance. These are the most-often ignored markings in band charts. Band members can get so wrapped up in playing the notes and being heard that they overlook one of the most sensitive aspects of musical interpretations. The trumpet section is usually too loud, the piano too soft, the guitar player gets carried away with his or her amp, and so on.

A famous conductor was invited to appear as guest conductor for a prominent concert orchestra. He arrived on time for the dress rehearsal to make his first appearance on that particular podium. The musicians welcomed him in anticipation of his appearance. He stood at the podium and looked around at the eager faces. He raised his baton and held it up for a moment. Then he said to the orchestra, "Too loud."

Dynamic Levels

The dynamic level markings shown below specify the volume to be played beginning at the measure where the marking appears. Following are the markings, their Italian names, and what they mean.

pp	*pianissimo*	very soft
p	*piano*	soft
mp	*mezzo piano*	medium soft
mf	*mezzo forte*	medium loud
f	*forte*	loud
ff	*fortissimo*	very loud

Measures 5, 13, and 17 in the example chart have dynamic markings.

There are also **ppp** and **fff**, at which point it gets ridiculous for a big band.

How loud is very loud, how soft is very soft, and everything in between? It's really a matter of interpretation by the individual musician and the band. As long as you agree and the music sounds right, it's right. The dynamic level changes reflect the relative difference between the loudest and the softest passages, and that audio dynamic range might vary depending on the size of the room, whether you're playing acoustic or amplified, the number of people in the audience, and whether they're noisy (like in a bar) or attentive (like in an auditorium).

*As the story goes, when jazz legend Louis Armstrong joined his first big band, he needed to learn the rudiments of reading music. In a rehearsal, the band was into a quiet passage and everyone was playing softly. Everyone except Satch, that is. He was taking the paint off the back walls with his trumpet. The leader stopped the tune and asked why Louis was playing so loudly. He said he saw the **pp** dynamic marking and thought it meant "pound plenty."*

Diminuendo and Crescendo

When the chart wants you to get quieter or louder, it will include *crescendo* and *diminuendo* marks as shown here in measures 12 and 16 of the example chart.

*teach yourself...*Jazz Piano Comping

The measures that follow such markings often include dynamic level markings to indicate how much louder or more quietly you should be playing. In the example you are playing *piano* (*p*) when you get to the *crescendo* at measure 12 and measure 13 is marked *mezzo forte* (*mf*). Measure 16 with the *diminuendo* goes from *mezzo forte* (*mf*) back down to *piano* (*p*).

The *diminuendo* and *crescendo* markings can span multiple measures.

These markings convey to the musicians what the arranger wants to hear with respect to dynamics. Sometimes you have to get quieter because the arrangement wants a gentler feel. Sometimes, because the band is backing a vocalist or instrumental solo or *soli*, the background music must not drown them out. Sometimes you have to play more loudly for your part to be heard over the band itself.

Try to observe and comply with the dynamic markings in an arrangement. You'll be one of the few.

Articulation

Articulation markings specify how you are to play specific chords. They override dynamic markings for the duration of that one chord and they can override the chord's duration itself.

Staccato

A *staccato* chord is marked with a dot above or below the notehead. With rhythmic notation, it's always above. But if you are reading a piano chart with keyboard notation, the *staccato* dot will be below those notes that have upward-pointing stems.

A chord marked staccato is played shorter than its notation would suggest. It is usually played at half the duration.

Measures 20 and 26 in the example chart contain *staccato* chords.

Accent

The *accent* marking specifies that you are to play the chord somewhat louder and with more attack than its neighbors. Then, for the next chord you return to the current dynamic.

teach yourself...Jazz Piano Comping

Measure 27 in the example chart contains two *accent* chords. This measure is an example of a *back beat*, in which the chords are played on beats two and four with rests on beats one and three.

Marcato

Marcato is similar to *accent* except that the volume is a bit louder and the attack is more prominent.

The example chart has no *marcato* chords, but they are often used.

Fermata

A *fermata*, also called a *birds-eye*, is placed over (or under in piano charts depending on the stem direction) a note or chord that is to be sustained, held longer than it normally would be based on its notation.

The *fermata* is often found on the last chord of ballads where an abrupt ending is not wanted. It allows vocalists and soloists to improvise an obbligato, which is a melodic line of indeterminate length inserted by a soloist.

Measure 30, the closing measure of the example chart, contains a *fermata*.

Other Articulations

There are other articulation markings, and if you encounter them, ask your buddies what they mean.

Expression

About the only *expression* marking you'll see in a big band piano chart is the RIT. mark which tells you to slow the tempo gradually. Here it is at measure 29 in the example chart.

The degree of slowing down is subject to the musicians' interpretation. Typically the leader will conduct the gradual tempo decrease.

*teach yourself...*Jazz Piano Comping

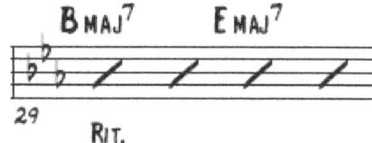

Key Changes

Key changes, also called *modulations*, are not something for you to absolutely have to worry about, since you're playing chords based on their symbols rather than from musical note notation. A C7 is a C7 no matter what key you are playing in. Nevertheless, it's helpful to know what key you are in. If the arrangement changes keys, there will be a new key signature looking something like this:

The flat or sharp symbols in the key signature for the previous passage that no longer apply are marked

natural (♮) and the new key signature follows. If some of the original signature's symbols continue, such as when you go from E♭ (three flats) to B♭ (two flats), only the one flat is marked natural in the new signature and the other two are shown like this:

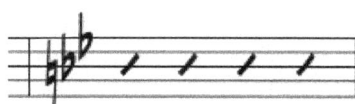

Why do you care about the key signature when the chart provides the chord symbols? Knowing the tonal center of the key you are in helps your mind find its place in the arrangement and reinforces your ear playing. That doesn't happen right off the bat, but with experience, "hearing" the next chord comes naturally.

A Walk Through the Chart

Given what we know about all the markings in this chart, let's take a walk, measure by measure, through *A Place Called Nowhere* as you would play it.

1. At the top, lay out for four measures while others in the ensemble play the intro.
2. At rehearsal number A, measure 5, make note of the left repeat sign and the Segno for future reference
3. Comp for seven measures.
4. At measure 12, bring the volume up slightly.
5. At rehearsal number B, play a bit more loudly for three measures.
6. At measure 16, bring it back down and play more quietly.
7. Play at measure 17, which starts the first ending, and play until measure 20.
8. After measure 20, return to the left repeat sign at rehearsal number A, measure 5.
9. Repeat measures 5 through 16.
10. Skip the first ending and proceed to the second ending, which begins at measure 21.
11. Play measures 21 through 24 up to and including the *D.S. al Coda* marking.
12. Return to the Segno at measure 5.
13. Iterate steps 3 through 10 above, putting you at the second ending.
14. Play measures 21 and 22 up to the Coda sign in measure 22.
15. Skip to the Coda which begins in measure 25.
16. Play through measure 28.
17. At measure 29, the *RIT* mark, begin to play more slowly, gradually reducing the tempo until the end of the arrangement at measure 30.
18. At measure 30, where there is a *fermata*, sustain the last chord until the leader signals to cut it off.

Exercise:

Sit at the piano, turn on the backing track (Appendix B), and play your first big band chart.

PART VI Playing

Part VI takes you beyond the role of chording pianist to introduce you to the worlds of comping, which is what this book is about, and improvisation. The discussion on comping addresses the rhythmic patterns that pianists use when they accompany other musicians. The discussion on improvisation introduces that topic and explains some of its basics, but does not provide complete coverage. Many books do just that and I encourage you to search your online bookstore for such titles.

Chapter 21. Comping Rhythms and Fills

Comping, for our discussion, is the playing of chords on and off the beat in a manner that states the harmonic context without playing a chord on every beat or maintaining a solid beat. It's what a piano player does during an instrumental solo or ensemble. It's what the guitar player can do when there's no piano player, or when you and the guitar player take turns comping. If you both comp at the same time, it's unlikely that you will be comping compatible rhythmic patterns. Typically, one of you lays out while the other comps.

The first thing you should do when you begin to study comping is to listen to other piano players doing it. They might play only one or two chords each measure. They play ahead of and after the beat. They sustain chords or play them *staccato*. Generally they make it up as they go, playing the correct chords but playing them when they want to, when to their ears it sounds best, a way to complement the soloist's lines and not get in the way.

You'll probably find that players have acquired a vocabulary of rhythmic patterns that they use. The patterns aren't dependent on the chords, only on the rhythmic nature of the accompaniment. The idea is to put the chords under the soloist or vocalist and to not interfere. Their solo is the feature. Your job is to pay attention to the solo, and insert chords and fills to make the solo sound good.

If there's a guitar player, don't comp with him. Either lay out or play rhythm piano in time and stay in the background.

To comp effectively, you must listen to the lines the soloist plays or the vocalist sings. You should know the tune's melody and its lyrics, too, if there are any. Then, you comp chords at places where the featured performance is quiet.

Of course, in a be-bop or scat solo, it's impossible to predict the next line, which means you have to listen. If you are familiar with the player, if you have worked with that player many times, it's easier. Otherwise, you need to know what the traditional improvisational idioms are in order to find your way through the choruses without playing intrusive accompaniments.

Rhythmic Patterns

Here are two choruses of *Blues in G*, with some alternate changes in rhythmic notation to show how you might comp for twenty-four measures.

Exercise:

Play the *Blues in G* backing track (Appendix B) and practice these rhythmic patterns.

Notice the rests, particularly the full-measure rests at measures 3, 13, and 15. These illustrate how you leave room for the soloist and that accompaniment doesn't have to fill every measure.

Fills

As you learned above, you generally stay out of the way when you accompany an ensemble, soloist or vocalist. You play minimalist chord patterns that state the harmony and rhythm, and do not interfere with the performance you accompany. There are places, however, particularly during the accompaniment of a single player or singer, when you can provide fills in the spaces that the featured performer leaves.

Fills are improvised lines that do what the name implies. They fill the silence left by the performer. They should fit the tune, be minimalist, and be melodic without actually playing the tune's melody—not your job.

Fills should not feature your technical skill. Listen to Oscar Peterson when he accompanies other players. The greatest technical jazz pianist alive at the time could blow everyone off the bandstand with his pianistic prowess. Yet he played conservative accompaniments.

Don't use Art Tatum as an example. He was the greatest jazz pianist ever, but his accompaniments in the recordings he made with others are all over the place. It works for him because he knew how to do it. No one else has ever figured that out, however.

Repetitious Comping

Up to now, in the book, you've learned a lot of chords and one way to voice each of them, all within the three-octave range that surrounds middle C, and fits on the bass and treble clefs of piano notation.

By now, you've played those chords over and over as you dealt with tunes, passages and changes. And maybe you feel like things are getting boring, the same chord voicing over and over.

How can you vary your chord voicings to keep you, your fellow musicians, and the audience from falling asleep? The obvious answer is to vary how you play each chord. Here are three methods you can apply to put variety into your comping:

- Alternate between rootless chords (Chapter 10) and chord voicings with root notes
- Play fewer notes than the complete chord calls for. They won't be missed in a sparse accompaniment.
- Vary the rhythmic patterns you use for comping
- Alternate playing inversions (Chapter 3) of the chords
- Move to different octaves for comping patterns. Higher usually works. Lower might sound a little thick. You'll determine what works with experience.
- Alter the dynamics of your accompaniments to match the dynamics of the tune. Get louder when the tune gets furious. Settle down during the more passive passages.
- Use any combination of the above

Of course, putting variety into your comping takes concentration and an application of what you know about harmonies and rhythms. It might seem difficult at first, but keep at it. Eventually, you'll be playing nice, varied accompaniments without thinking about it.

Chapter 22. Improvisation

Improvisation is the art of devising and playing extemporaneous melodies on the fly, melodies that match the harmonic context of the tune being played.

Improvisation is essential to jazz, but jazz isn't the only kind of music in which musicians improvise. Players of bluegrass, rock, lounge music, show tunes, chamber music, and all forms of pop music often employ degrees of improvisation in their performances.

This book does not teach improvisation. You can buy books that say they do, but I don't believe improvisation can be effectively taught with words. I'm not sure it can be taught with anything. It can be *learned* but it can't be taught, at least not by me. A teacher can expose you to the components of improvisation, some of which are described in this chapter, others of which are based in musical theory (Part III). After that, you're on your own.

The best way, in this writer's opinion, to learn improvisation is to first listen to those players whose improvisational skills you admire, and then try to play like them.

Some musicians have a natural aptitude for improvisation. They learn and improvise well-formed and pleasing lines much more quickly than some of their peers.

Some gravitate naturally to it without ever learning the formal terms and structure of music theory. Others never quite get the hang of it no matter how much they study. They learn the mechanics of improvisational theory—scales, arpeggios, licks, and so on—but they never figure out how to effectively apply that knowledge to their impromptu solos.

An improvisation must respect the rhythmic jazz feel of the tune being played. There are players who understand the concepts, the theory, and can play their instruments, but their time is not precise. They play what is called a "wiffle-waffle" style of improvisation. You have to nail the time. Hit the beats and the off-beats. Kick some butt. Don't be tentative or bashful. Play those lines.

That might lead you to conclude that you need a special gift and that without it, you'll never get past the most elementary levels of improvisation. Maybe so, maybe not. But gifted or not, you won't learn it without working for it. There is no silver bullet. It takes time, dedication and practice.

So, what exactly is improvisation?

Improvisation in jazz and other music genres can be described as spontaneous composition of melody lines based on known changes in a chosen style of playing.

That said, how do you compose in real time? It begins, of course, with knowing the tune. If you don't know the tune, or at least the chord changes, you probably can't improvise a new melody that fits. There are exceptions to this. Experienced horn players can hear the tune's chord changes as they are played by the pianist or guitar player, and lay down lines of new melody against the changes they hear. You are probably not there yet. And, of course, if you are told that the tune employs the changes of another tune you know, you can improvise on those changes without ever having heard the tune you're playing.

As a pianist you'll be playing both the improvised lines, usually with your right hand, and the changes, usually with your left, so you can't get away with not knowing the changes. Sorry, but that's just how it is.

Listen to the Improvisers

Pick a tune that you know and listen to other players improvise on it. If you listen to Art Tatum or Oscar Peterson you might be discouraged. Those guys are monsters. But don't try to be them. Just hear what they are doing and take from that what you can. The main thing you gain from lots of listening is your understanding of how good improvisation sounds.

Try to Improvise

Start up your backing track of the tune you were listening to (Appendix B) and try to play lines of improvised melody against the chord changes. Many jazz students begin with the blues (Chapter 14) and I suggest you do the same. Keep up with the line by comping chord fragments with your left hand.

The left hand chords don't have to be full voicings of the chords. You can play a couple notes that fit the chord and even leave out the root. The bass player has your bottom covered. If there's no bass player, put the root note on the bottom. Eventually, you'll learn when you can leave it out. Time and practice, like always.

Lines in this context are typically melodic passages that comprise one note at a time. The new melody line. Play only one note at a time as you improvise. There will be time enough later to learn to play lines and chords along with them. For now, keep it as simple as possible. And listen to the pros. Most piano improvisations, especially when there are other players in the rhythm section, employ one note lines much as a trumpet or sax player would do. And they add the left hand comping.

Play simple lines that include the chords' root notes and 5^{th}s. Just that. Get used to what they sound like. Add the thirds. Later you can fill in the other notes to form lines.

Play the *Blues in G*. Use a tempo with which you are comfortable. If 120 bpm is too fast, try 60. If that's too easy, try 90. And so on. For each measure, play a simple line that fits.

What fits? First, remember our number one rule.

If it sounds right, it's right.

All you have to do is play something that sounds right.

Yeah, I know, that's not a lot of help. So what can you improvise that you can be sure will sound right? What notes? What phrases?

Remember, listen to experienced players. Don't always try to copy them note for note. Try instead to be influenced by what they play.

Warning: Don't begin by trying to copy a free-form, inside-outside, chaotic chorus of dissonance and modal atonal scales. You aren't there yet. You might never be. That's okay with me.

Play simple lines that fit. Again, what fits?

Hum Your Improvisation

Try humming an improvised line against the chord changes. Don't worry about what notes you're humming other than that they fit the chords. Hum out loud what you hear in your mind. If you can hear it, you can hum it. Eventually, if you can hum it, you can play it.

Do this in small passages, only a few measures at a time. If you don't like what you hummed, hum something else. When you like what you hummed, try to play the notes on the piano. When you can play that line, hum something that fits the next several measures and learn to play that passage.

Now, how do you relate what you've heard, hummed, and played to the changes themselves? All you know is that the notes fit the chord changes, which means they sound right.

Match Notes and Chords

Determine the tonal center (Chapter 12) of the passage you are learning. If you're in a major key center, play notes from the major scale of that key. Not necessarily the scale itself, but notes chosen from that scale. Those will fit. Play those notes. Between beats, play what we call *passing tones*, notes that aren't in the scale but that pass chromatically from one scale note to another.

Playing Outside

Playing lines and going *outside* was popularized in the early 1960s by the new forms of modern jazz being played by Miles Davis, Bill Evans, and John Coltrane. It didn't start then and with those players. Art Tatum was going outside on the piano in the 1930s. Not many players tried to copy his style though, because his playing was way beyond anything they'd ever heard.

The outside idiom involves improvising lines based on the so-called *altered* scale of the current tonal center.

The altered scale of a dominant 7 chord is a seven-tone scale that contains the chord's root, 3rd and 7th notes. All the other notes are altered. For example, the C7 altered scale is:

C, D♭, E♭, E, F#, A♭, B♭.

Players go *outside* by playing lines based on this scale when the rest of the band is playing a C7 chord. The practice usually stays outside briefly and comes back inside shortly thereafter.

There is a way to go outside without trying to remember what's altered and what is not. Move the first note in the scale to the end and you have the D♭ harmonic minor scale shown here:

D♭, E♭, E, F#, A♭, B♭. C

To sound like you're playing outside, play a line a half-tone up from where you'd play it against the current dominant 7 chord. The E might become an F when you do that, but who cares? It's outside.

Don't forget to come back inside.

Blue Notes

There are many musical occasions other than playing outside when you can play notes not included in the tonal center's major scale, notes that are not passing tones. The notes you can play are called *blue notes*.

A blue note is a flatted 3rd, 5th, or 7th played in the context of the current tonal center. They're called blue notes because they fit especially well when you're playing the blues. They have a sad sound to them even in an up-tempo tune. They are like morphing into a sad minor key within the framework of a major key.

Flatted 3rd

The most recognizable blue note is the flatted third. Against a G chord, B♭ is that blue note. You would think the underlying chord would be G minor when the (improvised) melody note is a B♭ but it typically is not. The blue note in this context is similar to a raised 9th chord (Chapter 9), but it works with major chords as well as dominant 7 chords.

So the B♭ blue note can occur in a G major chord, a G7, a G7(♭9) and a G7(#9).

Flatted 5th

A flatted 5th is a form of bluesy dissonance when played against a major or dominant 7 chord, not to be confused with a tri-tone substitution (Chapter 17). The be-boppers discovered it as they searched for alternative and hip ways to improvise that didn't sound like traditional jazz and swing.

It became common for players to end a tune by playing the tonic's flatted 5th where the root note of the tonic was expected.

> *Eddie Condon, famous Dixieland guitar player, humorist, and bandleader, once said about be-bop jazz musicians, "They flat their fifths. We drink ours."*

Arpeggios and Scales

An arpeggio is playing the notes in a chord up and down. Look at any notated chord. Play the notes one by one, ascending up the chord. Then play them again, descending top to bottom. That's an arpeggio. Actually, it's two arpeggios.

You learned about scales in Chapter 2.

Knowing the tonal center (Chapter 12) of the current passage and how to arpeggiate and run scales are tools to use in making improvisations. They also help your ear know what note to play and where it is when your imagination dreams up a new line for your improvisation.

Conventional wisdom advises you to "arpeggiate up, scale down" when improvising.

Give it a try.

Licks

Licks are canned phrases that musicians use where the phrases fit. They can be as simple as a triplet and as complex as a series of jumps all over the keyboard.

All licks have this one thing in common: you've heard them before, perhaps not in the same place in the same tune, or with the same tonal center, but jazz musicians have heard them and recognize them.

Some licks are closely associated with well-known players, and if you use them, your fellow musicians on the bandstand will acknowledge your choice as being the "Parker" lick, or the "Montgomery" lick. Others are generic and everyone uses them. An example is the "Woody Woodpecker" lick, which contains a triplet arpeggio on the first beat of the lick and a pair of closing notes on the next beat. It got its name because the lick resembles the signature call that the cartoon character uses. *Dubada da-da!* It usually has a lead-in note to introduce the lick.

There are hundreds of licks, and hundreds of ways to use them. Listen for them in your jazz recording collection. When you hear what you think is a lick, write it down or play it on your piano. Then try it in different tonal centers.

A good way to improve your jazz lick vocabulary is from a book that teaches licks, and many such books are available. With a few licks under your belt, you are ready to amaze your pals at the next jam session.

It has been said that what separates a great jazz musician from an average one is how many licks each knows and how well they know to apply them in improvisations. A great player can play a concert without repeating a lick. But they're in the music nonetheless. Listen for them. Copy them. Add them to your jazz vocabulary.

Quotes

A popular form of lick is the *quote* wherein a musician inserts the notes of a passage from a different tune into what's being played at the time. Some quotes become clichés. Players quote the *Star Trek* theme in the first four bars of *Out of Nowhere* so often that it has become a standard part of any improvised solo on that tune. And they'll revel in their cleverness every time too, looking around to make sure everyone got it. Another worn out cliché is the refrain of *The Christmas Song* ("Chestnuts roasting...") inserted in place of the bridge for *Body and Soul*.

Some jazz musicians are eloquent with their quotes, inserting them where you'd least expect them. Others rely on the clichés or don't play quotes at all.

> *A band I played in for several years had a ritual for whenever anyone played a quote. They'd all pantomime pulling a chit from their pockets and writing it out. The chit was so you'd know you had to buy drinks for the band as penance for the quote.*

My friend and roommate on the road, the late Lou Mauro, a great bass player, used to complain that if he came up with a clever quote on the spot, all the players would be using it the following night. Of course, Lou complained about everything, but that's another story.

> *One night I quoted* Moon Over Miami *at the first four bars of* Perdido. *When it got around to the tenor player, he copied my quote. I told Lou about it later. He said, "Some guys can't even wait a day."*

Quotes can derail a tune.

> *I quoted* Ja-Da *as the intro to* Georgia on my Mind. *Or maybe it was the other way around. Half the band began playing one tune, the rest of the band was playing the other. The inevitable train wreck ensued. Wild Bill Davison, the leader, shook his finger at me when the tune was over and said, "Now that was your fault." He was right.*

Quotes are anathema to some musicians. If that musician happens to be the leader, quotes can get you in trouble.

> *The leader of a successful Dixieland band—some will guess the band right off; there aren't that many successful Dixieland bands—whose roots are planted firmly in traditional jazz, enforces an ironclad rule: no quotes. I asked one of his musicians whether everyone respects that rule to the letter. "Naw," he said. "We just quote tunes he wouldn't know."*

Impromptu Composition

This is the purest form of improvisation. You aren't thinking about chord changes or applying scales, arpeggios, licks or quotes. You are composing a fresh melody as you play. You hear the next note and you play it without consideration of where it fits in the harmonic context. You just know that it will sound okay.

> *Legend has it that in the studio for a recording session in 1947, Lionel Hampton was warming up at his vibraphones, running descending chromatic scales in an improvised harmonic manner. The engineer was setting up the tapes and recorded Hampton's exercises to get the levels right. Later they listened to the tape. Everyone agreed there was a song in there. Hamp added a bridge and the jazz standard,* Midnight Sun, *was born.*

There's not much more I can say about impromptu composition. Your skills as a composer grow with experience and practice.

Transcriptions

A *transcription* is an improvised solo that someone has put to paper so others can play it. I spent a lot of my childhood transcribing jazz solos from records. Then I'd memorize the solos. I still play some of them today just for the heck of it. They are great solos.

You don't have to laboriously write down transcriptions today. You can buy books of transcribed solos of your favorite jazz players. Many transcriptions are available online.

How do transcriptions help you learn to improvise? If you just use them as exercises in music reading and memorization, they don't necessarily instill in you the thought processes that the soloists used to come up with those solos.

You can eventually play a great player's solos note for note. But why do that? It's already been done. Be original when you perform.

That said, if you play transcriptions and think about the chord changes, you might get inside the head of the soloist. For this chord or change, this is what the soloist thinks, and so on. Then, rather than trying to play exactly like that soloist, you should be influenced by that player along with the influences of the other soloists you've transcribed and copied. Those influences, combined with what you bring to the exercises from your own imagination, will help you form your own voice.

Reward and Punishment

Every time you play a line that pleases you, that pleasure is a *reward*. Conversely, every time you play a line that displeases you, the displeasure is a *punishment*. These are the basic tenets of so-called *behavior modification*. Rewards are positive reinforcement of appropriate behavior. Punishment is negative reinforcement of inappropriate behavior. And by repeating the appropriate behavior and receiving the reward, you condition yourself to behave appropriately, thus learning to play good lines as a matter of habit.

Others can contribute to your rewards and punishment, and they can often do more harm than good. For example, you'll often hear musicians congratulate one another on their improvisations by saying things such as, "I hear you talkin', man." And they do it even when the chorus sucked. That's positive reinforcement of inappropriate behavior, it makes the player think he's doing okay, and he never improves. Maybe he'd never improve anyway, but unless his friends stop lauding his playing, he never *can* improve. If you don't want to give negative reinforcement to keep from hurting his feelings, at least withhold the positive vibes. Behavior ignored often becomes behavior abandoned.

If you don't like a line you've played, don't play it again just because you can. Just don't play it again. Repeat the lines you like. As you pile up the self-inflicted positive reinforcements, your behavior is subconsciously modified to be appropriate—to play good lines.

Chapter 23. Practicing

Face it. You have to practice. Your goal should be to make practicing enjoyable so that you'll be eager to escape to the practice room and get to it. Some of it will be repetitious and tedious and some of it will be fun. Work and play.

A musician on his first trip to NYC stops another musician on the street and asks, "How do you get to Carnegie Hall?"

The other musician answers, "Practice, man, practice."

That might be the oldest musician's joke known to the profession—its origins have never been established—but there is truth in the punch line. To be a proficient and successful musician, you must practice.

Concert pianist Vladimir Horowitz once said, "When I don't practice for a day, I notice. When I don't practice for two days, the orchestra notices. When I don't practice for three days, the audience notices."

There are as many approaches to a student's practice regimen as there are piano teachers, it would seem. If you have a teacher, by all means practice what he or she prescribes. But to get the most out of the lessons in this book, the best practice discipline in my opinion is this:

Play tunes

This should be obvious. Practice what you want to play, the tunes you like in the styles you want to learn. You can set aside time for scales, trills and arpeggios, but they alone are not what you'll be playing when you perform. They help build your chops but they don't teach you tunes.

Here are more guidelines in no particular order for you to develop effective practicing habits:

Tune up

Keep your piano in tune. If it's an electronic keyboard, no problem. If it's an acoustic, get a tuner in whenever you can hear slightly off-tune notes. Learning to play properly and by ear is far easier when the instrument is playing well, too.

Play in time

It's not enough to play the right chords. You have to play the right tempo, too. Every tune starts with a count-off. *One, two, one, two, three, four.*

Stick with the original tempo—the one you or the leader set up when you started playing the tune—and do not pause to find your way to a missed chord. Keep playing the tune and catch up where you can. You can return later to the troublesome passage and iron out the problem.

Remember, on the stand the band won't wait for you to find that elusive chord. A productive practice session teaches you not only the tune and its chords but how to play with discipline on the stand in front of an audience.

Playing in time also means maintaining a steady tempo. Do not rush or drag. If the drummer, bass player, or both are rushing or dragging, there's not a lot you can do other than complain. Time is everyone's responsibility. Some bass players play on top of the beat, which means they play their notes a fraction of a second before the beat. Don't chase them. Don't try to get on top with them. They'll adjust to get on top of your beat, and the tempo will be steadily rushed.

Exercise:

Select a tune that you know well, one with a medium tempo. Turn your recorder on. Kick off the tune but don't use a metronome or backing track. When you reach the end of the tune, listen to the beginning of the recorded tune and then move to the end. Are the tempos at either end of the tune consistent? If not, you need to keep working on time.

Repeat the exercise at various tempos.

What can you do if you're rushing or dragging the tempo? Try this:

Exercise:

Start your metronome at the troublesome tempo. Use a metronome that ticks audibly. You don't want beeps, you want ticks. Don't watch the metronome's pendulum if it has one. Now, clap along with the metronome. Try to clap such that your clapping drowns out the metronome's clicks. Every time you hear a click, your time is off.

Do this exercise many times at different tempos. Remember, you are a part of a *rhythm* section. Maybe you *are* the rhythm section. The band, the dancers, the audience, and whoever pays your wages depend on you to maintain a steady beat.

Learn the lyrics

If the tunes have lyrics, if they are *songs* in the literal definition of the word, learn the lyrics. Allow them to run in the back of your mind while you play the tunes. I know, you're concentrating on changes and tonal centers at the same time, but the lyrics are an integral part of the original musical composition, and if you know them, they will influence the lines that you improvise. If your listeners, even the ones with no formal musical education, can hear the song they know within the framework of your improvisation, you're doing it right. But if you can't hear it, they probably won't either. Thinking the lyrics while you play a song also helps you keep your place in the tune.

When you're not practicing, sing—in the shower, as you drive, wherever you can sound out without embarrassing yourself. Sing, sing, sing.

> *I was once driving through town with the windows open and singing* The Man I Love. *I got a lot of stares from other drivers and pedestrians. Be careful about where and what you sing.*

Use backing tracks

There are many sources for recorded or simulated backing tracks where a canned rhythm section plays through your stereo or your computer while you practice. You can search for them online, and you can use the ones that accompany this book as found on http://www.alstevens.com/jazzpianocomping.

Appendix B discusses the backing track software that I use and recommend.

Practice what you already know

We often hear that practicing what we've already learned won't help us advance. I disagree. In other disciplines it's called "review." In medical and legal professions, it's called "practicing" even when it's being done for clients as part of the profession.

Practicing what you already know serves two purposes. First, it gives you the confidence and positive feedback you get when you play something properly. Second, it reinforces earlier lessons and helps you retain and not forget them. So, take a break from the hard lessons at hand and play a tune or exercise you already know. You'll enjoy doing that, and, after all, learning is a lot easier when you have a good time doing it.

Practice two-chord changes

Pick a dominant 7th and a tonic, G9 and Cmaj7, for example, and practice that change repetitively. Try two beats per chord. Tap your foot with the rhythm. Go slow at first. Then as you become more accurate with the forms, speed up.

The idea is to get those forms into your muscle memory so that you don't have to think about them when they come up in a tune. Speak the chord symbol names as you play to get them into your subconscious memory, too, so you can associate each chord with its symbol, its sound, and its feel on the keyboard.

> *A musician's joke tells of when a fan requests* When Sonny Gets Blue. *The band singer doesn't know the tune. The piano player says, "I can sing it." So they kick it off. His vocal starts out like this:*
>
> *"When Sonny Gets Blue, B flat minor seven..."*

After you learn the first two-chord sequence, move your hand up a half-step, which in this case would be A♭7 and D♭maj7, reorient your fingers to the new chord's white and black key configuration, and repeat the exercise. Each day, practice the new position. Then finish off by practicing the change up and down the keyboard. Say the chord symbols when you play them.

Do not keep charts of these chords in front of you all the time that you practice. All that does it make you dependent on the charts. You want to learn what the music sounds and feels like, not what it looks like.

Practice three-chord changes

With the two-chord changes under your belt, add the two-minor-seven chord at the front and practice those ii-V-I three-chord changes up and down the keyboard (Chapter 13).

Look at the charts

Don't look at the keyboard all the time. When you are reading charts with a band, you need to keep your eye on the chart so you know the changes you are expected to play, the navigation of the chart, and so that you don't get lost in the arrangement.

Look away from the charts

This teaches you to play tunes without relying on the charts. It's also necessary if you are accompanying yourself on vocals to be able to play while you sing and pay attention to the audience. Again, don't look at the keyboard any more than is absolutely necessary.

Read ahead

When reading charts, whether they be lead sheets, chord charts, or big band charts, whether they be in slash, rhythmic, standard notation, or some combination, it's important that you read ahead of yourself. This comes with practice, but if you don't practice doing exactly this, it will never come.

Begin by looking at the first measure. Remember, unless you are soloing, you are interested only in the chords and the rhythmic patterns of your comping. Put the first measure to memory. Then, as you play the first measure from memory, read and put to memory the second measure. Read ahead like that for the entire chart.

It's not easy at first. It takes a bit of a split personality. Your conscious mind concentrates on the next measure while your subconscious mind plays the current one.

Being able to do this is the first step to learning to *sight read*, to read a chart at near performance levels the first time you see it. It's an ability you'll need in order to play in a big band.

When you can comfortably read charts by looking a measure ahead, expand your scan to two measures ahead, which you assimilate while you are playing the current two.

It is helpful to realize that eventually, each measure you look at will often be a chordal and rhythmic pattern you've seen countless times before. You'll see a sequence of the 1,6,2,5 changes, for example, and know immediately how to play all four chords and how to move from one to the other. Naturally, that takes experience and practice.

When you are able to read ahead two measures at a time, expand your scan to four.

Time will come when you look at a many-measure passage or even a whole chart beginning to end, and realize that you already know the complete set of chord changes in the key being shown. You'll say, "aha, rhythm changes," or "eureka, Sears Roebuck bridge," or "got it, blues changes," and so on. (You probably won't really say, "eureka.")

The only way to get there, though, is with practice. Lots of it.

Learn each tune in several keys

Use your backing track software (Appendix B) to change the key several times of each tune that you learn. Become familiar with the usual keys for jazz music. The usual jazz keys are C, E♭, F, G, A♭, and B♭, with an occasional departure into D♭. Few jazz tunes are in the keys that country players are used to: A, D, E, and G, and less often, B. One prominent jazz tune in D is the bossa nova, *Wave*. Learn that tune in D and you can mostly ignore the key for all the other tunes. Sometimes singers will request an unfamiliar key. You can usually slide them up or down a half-tone to put the tune where it will be comfortable for the rest of the band.

Listen to other piano players

This is important. Devote a good portion of your study to the works of others, the players you'd like to emulate. Listen to how they thread their playing through the changes and substitutions. Call their performances up on YouTube and watch them play. Make note of the tunes they play that you like and add those tunes to your list of tunes to learn.

Have a place to practice

It's best to have a quiet, isolated practice room, preferably one in which you won't be interrupted and your practice won't interfere with the lives of others. Everybody's situation is different so I'll leave it to you to set yourself up with a workable studio.

> *The piano I learned on as a boy in the 1950s was in the room next to the living room where the family watched TV. I was not allowed to practice when anyone was watching the tube. To improvise my own makeshift soundproof studio, I hung sheets of newspaper between the hammers and the strings on our upright piano. This muffled the notes to a pitter-patter that was deemed acceptable to the others. I couldn't tell whether the pitch was correct, but my scales and arpeggios benefited from the modification. Whatever works.*

Use comfortable tempos

Set the playback of the backing track (Appendix B) for a tune to a tempo with which you can keep up. As you get comfortable with the slower tempo, speed it up. Do that until you're playing the tune at performance tempos.

Repeat difficult passages

If you run across a difficult passage that needs attention, use the backing track software (Appendix B) to loop it so you can concentrate on problem spots until the problems go away.

Keep your interest alive

If you get bored with a tune, set it aside and practice another one. Nothing discourages the learning of an intricate art form as much as tedium. It's why so many players object to practicing scales.

Practice a lot

I won't try to tell you how many hours a day you should practice. That's up to you. Not everybody has all the time in the world. Most people—even piano players—have lives. Some teachers recommend practice sessions of no more than fifteen minutes. If that works for you, fine. But bear in mind the 10,000 hour rule, which maintains that it takes 10,000 hours of deliberate practice to become a world-class practitioner in any field. Be grateful that playing the piano is a labor of love. Practicing might become tedious, though, so use your practice time wisely to achieve an even balance of skill-building and enjoyment.

Don't overdo it

If your hands or arm joints or muscles hurt, give it a rest. Take your hands off the keyboard and flex them. Pushing an injured or strained body part past its limits can do serious damage and end your playing career. If you're tired, get some sleep. Eat properly. Drink lots of water. Don't smoke, even when you're not practicing. Leave the recreational drugs out of your practice regimen. They'll just make you think you're playing better than you are.

Involve other musicians

This is an important aspect to productive practicing. Whenever possible, get together with other players to "shed" your music. Whether you congregate in a garage, busk on the street for tips, or attend public jam sessions, make sure you include other musicians as part of your learning process. You'll learn faster if the other musicians are better than you. Lots better. You rise to the challenge, and more experienced players can and will mentor you and show you the ropes.

Appendix A: Chords

This appendix summarizes the chords you've learned in *teach yourself... Jazz Piano Comping*, and it provides each chord for all twelve root notes. There is only one suggested voicing for each chord but you are not restricted to that voicing. Try the chord at hand in different octaves, with different inversions, and by omitting a note or two while you comp.

Basic Chords, Chapter 4

These are the four basic chords upon which all other chords are built.

Colorful Dominant 7 and Minor 7 Chords, Chapter 5

These are the dominant 7 and minor 7 chords with 9th and 13th intervals added to give the chords a more colorful sound.

Colorful Major and Minor Chords, Chapter 6

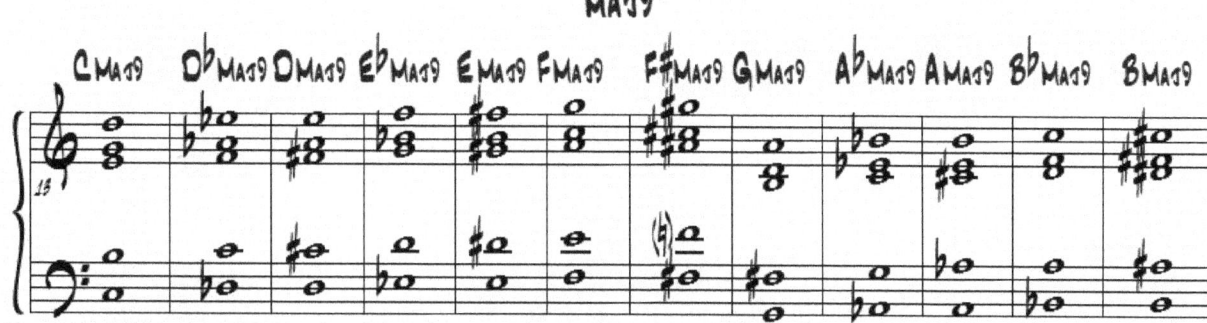

teach yourself...Jazz Piano Comping

Colorful Major and Minor Chords, Chapter 6 (continued)

Colorful Major and Minor Chords, Chapter 6 (continued)

Diminished Chords, Chapter 7

These are the diminished chords.

The first four of the diminished 7 chords are really all the diminished 7 chords there are. The other eight are inversions of the first four. See Chapter 7 for details.

The half diminished chords are also minor 7 chords with flatted 5^{th}s, thus the two names for them.

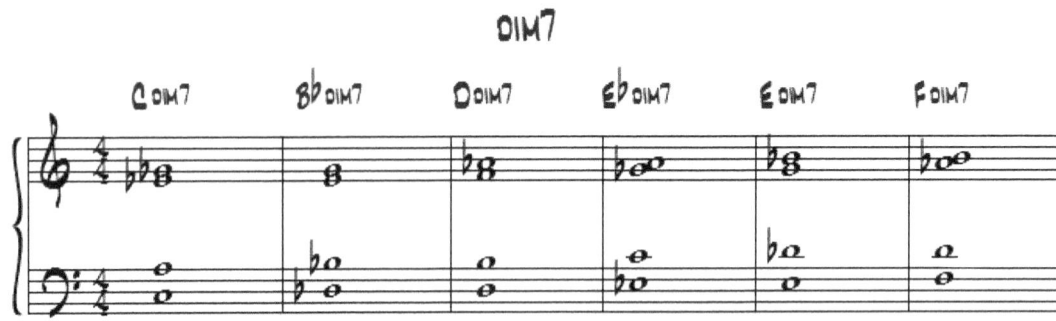

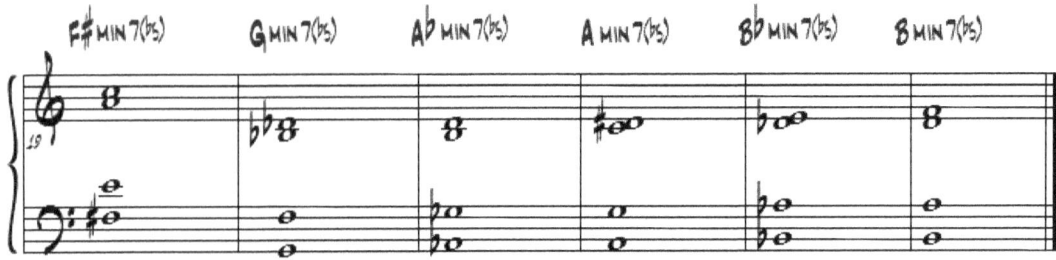

Augmented Chords, Chapter 8

These are the augmented chords.

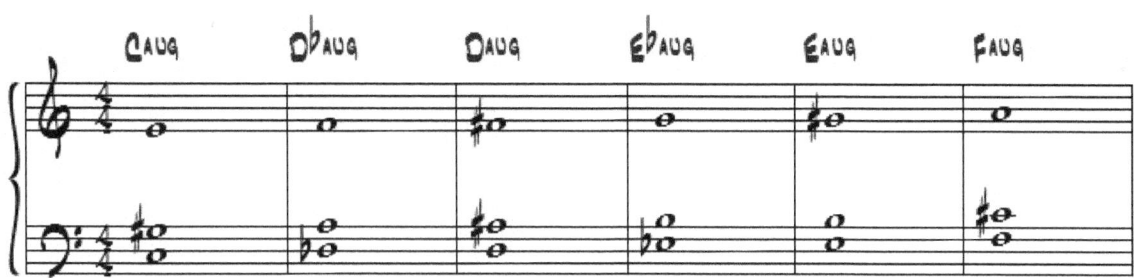

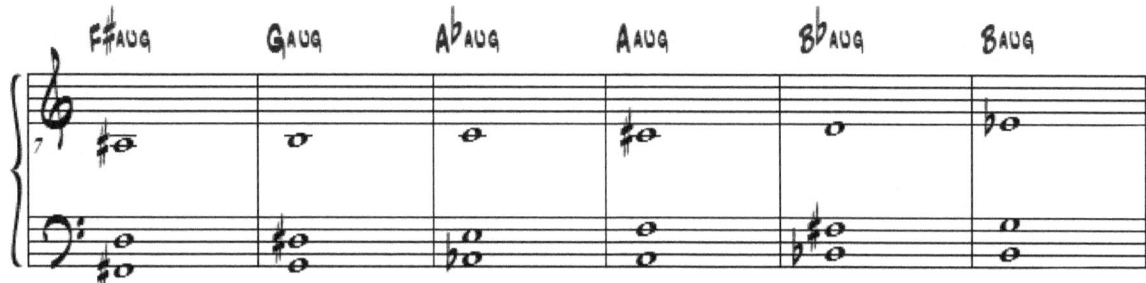

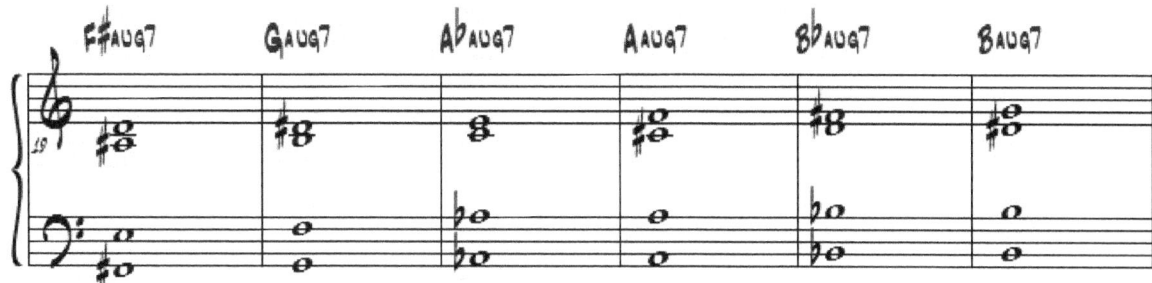

Suspended Chords, Chapter 8

These are the suspended chords.

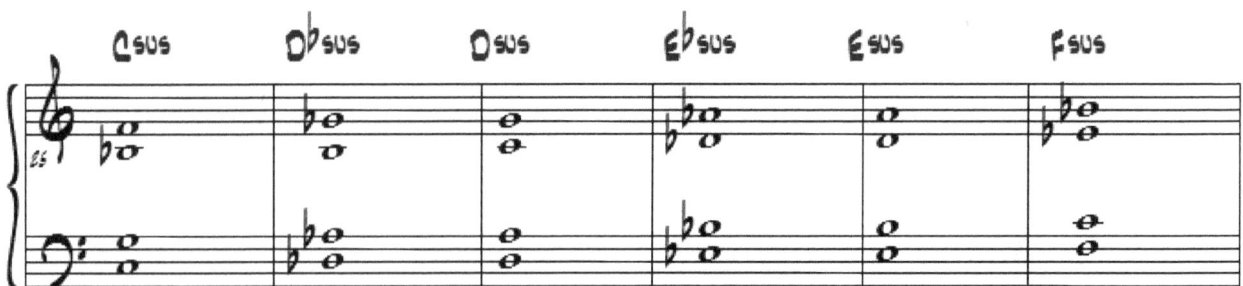

Altered 9th Interval Chords, Chapter 9

These are the sharped and flatted 9th chords.

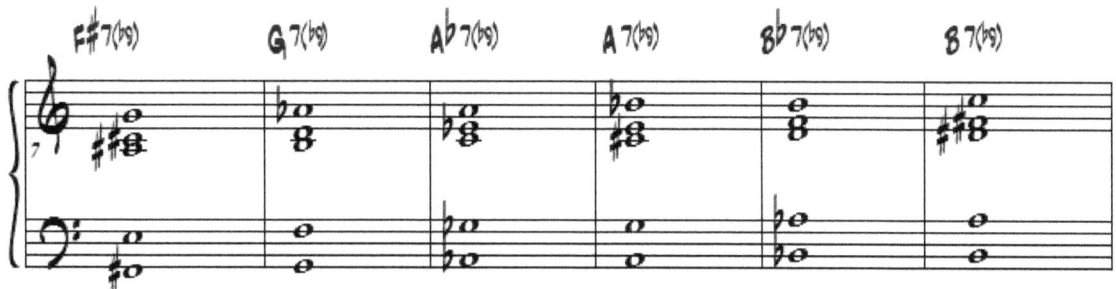

Altered 5th Interval Chords, Chapter 9

These are the infamous flatted 5th chords.

Appendix B: Got Software?

You can follow this book cover to cover using only your piano, and you can learn what this book has to teach that way. The exercises stand alone. But the practice tunes can be much easier to learn when you have the assistance of a rhythm section.

If you can afford to hire a drummer and bass player to drop by when you want to practice, by all means, go for it. Most of us can't do that. For us there are backing tracks.

Backing tracks are recorded rhythm sections with which you practice. They provide a rhythm section and leave out the solo instrument. The first known of these are the old Music Minus One records originally released in the 1950s as sing-along and play-along recordings of popular tunes. Musicians would use the records that omitted the instrument (or vocal) that they wished to play along with. Probably the best known of such products are the Jamey Aebersold Play-A-Long Series.

Some performers use backing tracks when performing so they don't have to hire a rhythm section. As piano players, we should object to that. Except that some piano players use backing tracks to provide bass, guitar, and drum accompaniment. That's okay. Unless you play bass, guitar or drums.

A more recent generation of backing tracks is found in Karaoke technology which provides not only the accompaniments but the lyrics projected on a screen for the benefit of amateur singers who patronize Karaoke operators. You won't find that to be of much help when you practice piano comping.

Band-in-a-Box

Probably the most widely used backing track technology and the one I use is a computer program named *Band-in-a-Box*® (BIAB) available from:

http://www.pgmusic.com

If you use BIAB, you may download the free practice backing tracks from my website at:

http://www.alstevens.com/jazzpianocomping.

This Appendix is not a tutorial on the use of BIAB. Instead, I'll explain how I use it. You can find all the help you need in online tutorials and discussion groups at YouTube and the pgmusic website.

Here's BIAB with the old standard *Blue Moon* loaded and ready to play. As you can see, the user interface is complex. This screen shot doesn't show most of it.

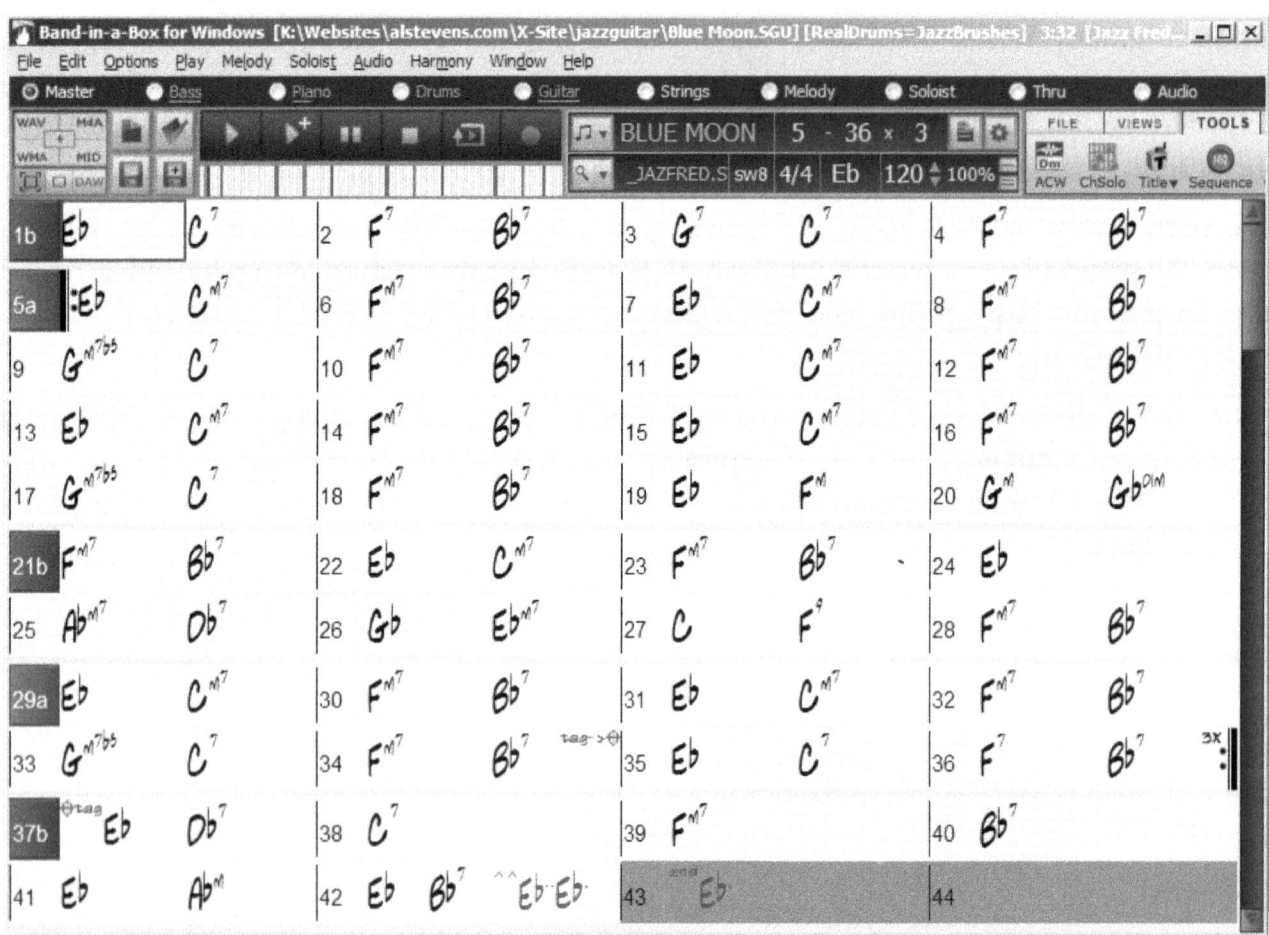

The program itself doesn't come with many tunes, but you can find them on the Internet and ones that go with these lessons on my website at http://www.alstevens.com/jazzpianocomping.

You can load a backing track or manually key in the chords for a tune, and build a track of your own. You can change the key, the tempo and the style in which the tune is played. You can adjust the volume and pan of each instrument in the ensemble that the backing track employs.

You can program intros, tags, repeated choruses, interludes, virtually anything you can do with a live band to practice with.

Many of the BIAB styles use the playing of real musicians by mapping their riffs and chords to the tune's chord structure. You can even design and implement your own styles.

Because I play piano and bass, I used to record my own backing tracks for standard tunes and I'd use a BIAB-generated drum track for drums. I used those tracks to practice sax, trumpet and trombone. With the latest versions of BIAB, I no longer do that. Its real-time accompaniments play piano and bass well enough that I don't need the realistic sound of my own playing. I haven't used those homegrown tracks in several years now.

As far as I know, Band-in-a-Box® is the only program on the market that delivers all that a practicing musician needs in the way of personal accompaniment—short of a live rhythm section, that is.

> *Disclaimer: I have no financial interest in the BIAB product. The company that owns and distributes it is aware of this endorsement and has provided me with the latest version to facilitate this discussion.*

Appendix C: Jazz Jargon

These are terms and phrases you'll hear tossed about in the studio, on the bandstand, on the band bus, wherever jazz musicians hang. Some of them are affected, some are antiquated, going back sixty years or so. But here they are so you can keep up with what your peers are saying.

ax	A musician's instrument
bad	good
bandstand	the stage where you perform
beat	a measure of rhythm
big band	an ensemble of about 16 musicians that plays jazz and swing arrangements
blow	play jazz
bone	trombone
bop	a style of jazz developed in the 1940s
break	a pause in a tune during which one musician plays
bring us in	count off the tune's rhythm
cat	musician
change	a chord
changes	a sequence of chords
chart	an arrangement, lead sheet, or chord sheet
chick singer	female vocalist
chops	a player's endurance and stamina to play the instrument
clam	a harmonic or melodic error that stands out
combo	a small band consisting of a rhythm section and zero or more horns
comp	accompany
cool	good, pleasing
dig	like, appreciate
drag	slow down the tempo
fills	improvised lines that you play to fill the space in a soloist's rendition.
free	a form of jazz that does not adhere to structure of any kind
front	an insert for the stand to identify the band
ghost band	name band of which the famous leader is deceased and the band continues to perform
hack meter	play too many or too few beats in a measure
head	the main refrain of the tune, the chorus
head arrangement	memorized format for the musical rendition of a tune

teach yourself...Jazz Piano Comping

hip	savvy, knowledgeable
house band	the band employed by the venue to accompany featured performers and those sitting in
intro	musical introduction to a tune's performance
jam session	gathering of musicians to play ad hoc and impromptu tunes
kack	die
kick it off	count off the tune
lay out	refrain from playing during part of a tune's performance
lead sheet	a chart of a tune's notation with chord symbols and a single-staff melody line
lick	a recognized harmonic, melodic and rhythmic pattern inserted into an improvisation
licorice stick	clarinet
mainstream	jazz based on standard popular tunes played in commercial styles
man	a name with which to address a musician
mother key	F
number	tune, so called because charts in a part's folder are numbered
obble-gobble	Obbligato, refers to an important accompanying part which is not to be omitted
out chorus	the last chorus of a tune's performance
outside	a style of improvisation that uses the altered scale against a dominant 7 chord
pocket	groove
play the ink	play a band chart as it was originally published and ignore manual (pencil or ink) markings
riff	an improvised ensemble pattern played behind a soloist
road map	the navigational properties of a band chart
rush	speed up the tempo
scat	improvised vocal lines with meaningless words
shed	practice a tune or a program of tunes
sit in	play as an unpaid guest with a house band
smooth jazz	a style of jazz with little or no improvisation that sounds weak and pointless to real musicians
stand	a rack for holding charts on the bandstand
swing	v. play in the pocket or groove. n. music that swings
trad	traditional jazz, usually Dixieland
train wreck	a musical mishap that ruins the tune's performance
turnaround	a passage that provides the transition between other passages
woodshed	practice

From the Author

Thank you for reading *teach yourself*...Jazz Piano Comping.

If you enjoyed this book—or even if you didn't—please visit the site where you purchased it and write a brief review. Your feedback is important to me and will help other readers decide whether to read the book.

If you'd like to get notifications of new releases and special offers on my books, please join my email list at http://www.alstevens.com.

Al Stevens, 2018
al@alstevens.com

About the Author

Al Stevens is a retired author of computer programming books. For fifteen years he was a senior contributing editor and columnist for Dr. Dobb's Journal, a leading magazine for computer programmers.

Al lives with his wife Judy and a menagerie of cats on Florida?s Space Coast where he writes by day and plays piano, guitar, string bass, and saxophone by night.

www.ingramcontent.com/pod-product-compliance
Lightning Source LLC
Chambersburg PA
CBHW050749100426
42744CB00012BA/1940